There's Something about Mary

Conversations with Irish Women Politicians

Mary Banotti

CURRACH
PRESS

For Geraldine Green,
with thanks and admiration

Thanks to:
Geraldine Green
Nora Owen
Mary Challinor
Jo O'Donoghue
John Fanagan
Tania Banotti

Contents

Introduction

I was born in Blackhorse Avenue near the Phoenix Park in Dublin. I try sometimes to remember what it was like to be 'an only child' but I think my memories are based on old family photos. I see a sturdy rather solemn child with a thick fringe of black hair standing in the long back garden or sitting on my mother's knee at picnics – she looks happy in a way I can no longer remember. She was Kitty Collins and she had married in 1937. My dad, Jim O'Mahony, met her at a garden party in Dublin. One of his pals had said to him, 'I dare you go over and get off with that starchy one,' and he did and totally uncharacteristically for her at least, they were engaged a fortnight later.

Mother was a serious, rather imposing person. Her sisters never believed she would be married. Her elder sister Mary was a jolly extroverted girl, who was by all accounts better-looking and was always asked up to dance while my mother sat it out. Hence the surprise when she met and married my father, who had been born in England, son of a customs officer under the British authorities. His mother, my godmother, Elizabeth Potter, had trained as an actress with Henry Irving in London. My father had also attended the Abbey School of Acting and was honourably mentioned in Lady Gregory's *Diaries*. His sister Nora was an actress too and ended her career as a national figure playing Godmother in *Wanderly Wagon*.

My dad worked in the National Bank – most actors in those

days had to have what was always referred to in our house as 'a real job'. In the 1940s Daddy appeared in a series of British films made in Ireland. We were told that the English actors loved coming to Ireland, where they could escape the grim, post-war Britain. Why do I always remember porterhouse steaks at that time? Daddy had bit-parts in character roles in *Odd Man Out, I See a Dark Stranger* and *Captain Boycott*. Every so often these old films turn up on TV and I have to scan them carefully to see him. He always seemed to be cast as a Garda, a bus conductor or a station master. His long funny face looked interesting in a peaked cap. My mother loved the excitement and glamour of this side of Daddy's life and she regularly entertained Abbey actors who in time became very well known.

When I was two we moved from Blackhorse Avenue to Clontarf. When we arrived in Stiles Road our house was the last in a row of eight semi-detached houses. Around us were green fields and behind the back wall a mysterious demesne; seen through the thick trees was Clontarf Castle. Sometimes we would climb over the wall and creep through the undergrowth, terrified by the dark shadows. We grew up in a normal family: roller-skating on the road, riding our bikes, going to school, listening to the radio. In summer we travelled to visit my mother's sister Mary Pierse in Listowel, or to the Curragh Camp to stay with her other sister Joan Bunworth, whose husband Dick taught in the Military College.

The Curragh holidays were when I began to understand that boys were different and very interesting. I was whistled at while walking down the centre of the Camp, with hundreds of young soldiers hanging out the windows. It was bliss.

By January 1949 there were five – one boy and four girls – in our family, with a live-in housekeeper. That was when life took on a dark frightening feeling. My father very suddenly started to lose his sight. He was in and out of hospital having multiple operations as doctors tried to find out the cause of his condition. No one talked to young children about these issues.

I experienced true fear for the first time. Daddy was now wearing dark glasses and spending all his time at home. In May 1949 my youngest sister Joan was born. When we went in to visit her in the nursing home Daddy dropped a box of chocolates on the bed which hit the baby because he couldn't see her. It was an omen of things to come. My mother, a deeply religious woman, coped by going to Mass every morning. We resisted as best we could the early-morning pressure to go with her.

In October of that year Daddy was in hospital yet again. One morning I awoke early and was overwhelmed with fear and dread. I knew he was dead. I turned to go back to sleep and did so hoping that when I awoke again things would be different. They weren't. I got up and went out of my room, ignoring our housekeeper who told me to go back to bed. I said, 'I am going to Mass,' and I saw her horrified face as I left the house. She said our absent mother had told her that we were to stay in bed. Already this confirmed for me that something was terribly wrong. I went to the church and after the Communion the priest, who didn't know I was there, turned around to the small local congregation and announced my father's death. I started to howl and a kind neighbour quickly took me home.

For sixty years I have never ceased to feel the pain and grief of that day. I was ten years old, the eldest of six children, in my mind castigating my father for leaving me alone with my mother, who was also suffering.

My mother was thirty-eight. It was many years before I was able to begin to understand the appalling challenge that faced her then. I am the only one in the family who remembers our father and in some ways that separates me from my much-loved brother and sisters. In contrast, they understood our mother better than I did.

She, Kitty Collins, had an extraordinarily traumatic childhood. Her father, Johnny Collins, lived near Sam's Cross, Clonakilty, in west Cork. His youngest brother Michael became a national hero, whose life has been well documented. Kitty's mother had been suffering from miliary tuberculosis ('galloping consumption') and died in February 1921. Shortly afterwards, in April 1921, the homestead was burnt down by Crown forces and, on the same day, Johnny was arrested and interned in Spike Island. With her mother dead and their home destroyed, my mother and her seven siblings were split up for a time among various relatives.

The family was thus caught up in the drama of Ireland's fight for independence and the subsequent assassination of Michael Collins during the Civil War. My mother was among the last to see Michael alive when he briefly stopped to visit his family on 22 August 1922. As he left, he bent down to kiss my mother goodbye and she protested, saying, 'I'm nearly twelve now and I'm too old to be kissed.' Two hours later he was dead at Béal na mBláth.

In September 1922, my mother and her eldest sister went away to boarding school in the Dominican Convent, Wicklow. In 1923 my grandfather remarried. His second wife was a wonderful woman, Nancy O'Brien, who became a much-loved stepmother and grandmother.

When I think of the trauma experienced by many families at that time I marvel how they were ever able to cope with all that loss and grief. But while I was growing up I was not able to understand the effects of that time on my mother. I believe that what kept her going was an intense sense of duty, a deep religious faith and the courage which so characterised her family. However it did not make Kitty Collins easy to love or to live with. I was now 'the eldest', in charge of the younger children. I learned to cook, just plain cooking. I have no particular memories of fun or warmth at that time and after two years it was almost a relief to be sent away to the same boarding school my mother had attended. My four sisters followed me.

From an early age I always wanted to 'go and tour the world'. Instead I was enrolled in a commercial college with a view to joining the bank where my father had worked. As the daughter of a former official I was soon employed. I spent eight months shoving cheques into pigeon holes in the head office in College Green. It was agony. I was expected to help financially at home and this added to my guilt. Eventually I plotted my escape, aided by an English cousin. I would develop a vocation to be a nurse, which was a highly respected profession, and go to an English hospital where board and keep and modest wages would be included in the training. All this happened and thus I came to live a geographically separate life from my family.

In England I really felt I was on my own. Nursing training in the London Hospital was tough and I was the first Irish trainee they had admitted. While I will always be grateful for the excellent training I received, my gratitude is qualified by my sense of the anti-Irish prejudice which I found there. I was not a natural nurse but the lack of other choices made me persist to the end of the training. One Saturday during this time I went down the Portobello Road in Notting Hill. While having a cup of tea in a sleazy café I met a delightfully shady-looking man with a very respectable wife. We chatted for a while and he asked if I would like to run one of his stalls, selling antiques. I was thrilled. For the next year I worked night-duty in the hospital every Friday and all the next day in the now famous market. There I fell in love for the first time with the guy at the next stall. He had a parrot on his shoulder and a beard, and was definitely every mother's nightmare for her daughter. In any case, the passion was not sufficient to prevent me pressing ahead with my plans to tour the world.

For the next twelve years after leaving Dublin I lived in five countries: England, Canada, the USA, Africa and Italy. In 1967 I married in Italy, where my daughter Tania was born. Following the collapse of my marriage I returned to Dublin in October 1970, arriving on the day after Charlie Haughey was acquitted in the Arms Trial. By this time, thanks to my travels, I had had a ringside view of the genesis of the Civil Rights Movement in the US and had been in Kenya at the end of colonial rule.

In Dublin the women's liberation movement was just starting. It was an exciting time. There were so many real issues for the women's campaigns: equal rights, family home protection, family violence. Through the Women's Political Association there was a push to elect more women both to the Dáil and local councils. The next decade saw Nuala Fennell, Monica Barnes and of course my sister Nora Owen elected to the Dáil. The day Nora was first elected, in June 1981, was one of the happiest of my life.

I was by this time working in the distilling industry as a welfare officer and I helped to establish the Women's Aid hostel in Harcourt Street and the Rutland Treatment Centre. All these experiences were hugely useful when I was later elected as a Member of the European Parliament. In the autumn of 1983 George Colley died unexpectedly and there was a by-election in Dublin Central. I was selected as the Fine Gael candidate in what proved to be an extremely tough campaign. It was the first election in which Dublin voters experienced the influx of Sinn Féin canvassers from Northern Ireland at this difficult time in North–South politics. I was defeated by Fianna Fáil's Tom Leonard, a gentle nice man. At the count in Bolton Street I experienced the 'aggro' that often characterises counts at by-elections and as I was being barracked by Fianna Fáil supporters, Charlie Haughey silenced them by leaning back and swiping out at them, for which I was very grateful.

In 1984 I was selected to run with Richie Ryan as a candidate for the European Parliament. To our great delight we were both elected. I remember the day after the count waking up at home in Ringsend and lying in bed thinking, my God, I am elected, what do I do next? It was some days before I received the call to come out to Brussels.

My time in the European Parliament was very satisfying personally. I have made friends from all over the world and found the work in the Parliament totally absorbing. I was appointed to the environment committee and saw the evolution of European environmental policy which has been of such huge importance. My work in the Parliament gave me the opportunity to travel widely. I was still in effect 'touring the world', observing elections in many countries over the years.

There were few women in the Parliament when I was elected and all of us were over the age of forty. None of us had young children, most of us had strong political backgrounds and all of us were determined to take our places in the many responsible positions open to Members. I was conscious, particularly among my Irish fellow-Members, of being in a minority in a strongly male world. I did enjoy the camaraderie of male colleagues from all the political groupings but at times I needed to call them to task. Most obliged with good humour and fun.

By the time I left in 2004 there were many more women, both young and old, several crèches and no need any longer to emphasise the equality agenda: it was taken as read.

In 1997, I was nominated as the Fine Gael candidate to run for the Presidency of Ireland after the term of Mary Robinson. Mary had brought a totally new dimension to the role of President. The election took place at the end of October that year. There were four other candidates, three of whom were women – Mary McAleese, Dana Rosemary Scallon, Adi Roche and Derek Nally. This was a mixed blessing as it now seemed that the job would become so feminised that it was in danger of becoming devalued. However after a memorable campaign Mary McAleese was elected, and in 1994 she was re-elected unopposed.

In 1995, as a member of the petitions committee in the European Parliament, I was appointed the Parliament's Mediator for Transnationally Abducted Children. In 1993, there had been a dramatic march to the Parliament in Strasbourg by hundreds of women whose children had been removed by their fathers to North African countries. These mothers, in many cases, had never been able to see their children again or bring them back to where they had been born, in France, Belgium or the Netherlands. I have been doing that work since and, having had a personal experience of abduction, I felt qualified to raise this issue and to participate in the drafting of amendments to the Hague Convention, which is the critical international law governing this issue.

In 1999, I topped the poll among the MEPs and was elected one of five Quaestors. Quaestors represent the members in the governing body – the 'Bureau' – of the Parliament. I continued in this role until 2004, which gave me an interesting insight into the background activities of the Parliament. During my last two-and-a-half years as an MEP, Pat Cox served as the first Irish President of the Parliament, and made an enormously positive contribution in that office. In 2004, after twenty years, I decided that this was long enough for anyone in politics, and that I would not present myself again for re-election. Following my final session in the Parliament, which was both happy and sad, I took off for America to observe the second election of George W. Bush – but that's another story.

In my class at school in the 1950s there were eleven girls, six of whom were called Mary. As a result we Marys were forever fated to carry two names or even a nickname to distinguish one from another. We lived in a culture of Mariology. We were all the eldest girl in our families and we all believed we were called after the Virgin Mary. We even had the month of May as our special time.

In Ireland at that time almost all education for girls was provided in convent schools and each nun had the name Mary before her name in religion. Consequently we believed that we were blessed in a particular way. Rebukes for wayward behaviour generally included reference to the fact that the Virgin Mary would not approve of such behaviour.

Nowadays, children are inclined to believe that all Presidents of the country are called Mary! A significant number of Oireachtas members bear the name as well.

When I embarked on this 'Marianesque' project I hoped to find out what unites all the political Marys and what drives us to take the risks that are essential for success. Why do so many Marys emerge from a variety of families to take their place in public life in a country that had so few women in public life until relatively recently?

I have interviewed most of these Marys and it proved to be a most pleasurable exercise. We all had the common experience – some would say nightmare – of elections, public campaigns, caution about the media, experience of failure and backbiting, family pressures and profound relief when elections were successfully over.

No one who has not had the multiple experiences of political life – constituency conventions, attendances at political gatherings (almost *de rigueur* to be held in dank, depressing pubs or halls), the smell of fear when support drifted to other candidates; the terror of speaking to members of your own Party (which far outweighs campaigning among the general public) – can imagine what these experiences are like. They toughen and tenderise those who go through them and the experience of failure can be traumatic indeed, particularly for women. I know that men also dread these times, but, in my opinion, women tend to take them more personally and, if they fail, have difficulty in coming back for more.

The majority of the Marys are now over forty years of age. Only three have young children and most have no children. This collection of interviews seeks to provide a snapshot of the personal and political lives of these courageous women.

I thank all the Marys for taking the time to talk to me as entertainingly as they did in the midst of very busy lives. Without exception, they have made significant contributions to the life of our country.

So that I would know how it feels, the final interview in the sequence is with myself. It was conducted by my schoolteacher friend and literary mentor, John Fanagan.

Mary Coughlan

You're the eldest in your family.
The eldest of seven. I have five brothers and a sister.

Just to get the Mary bit out of the way, do you know why you were called Mary?
I never really asked but I assume it is because my mother's name is Marian. I was born in 1965 and Mary was a very popular name for lots of girls. My mother's name was Mary Ann but she was known as Marian.

Were there many Marys in your school?
A good few, yes. We would have had far more than now. When I reflect on my daughter's class or even her school I'm sure there are no Marys – that's as far as I recall.

It was a traditional Irish name.
Yes, and I think that is the only reason it would have been common enough at that time.

None of you were given what we now call fancy names?
No, all the names in our house were traditional. We would have been named after grandads, grannies, apart from Ian which is a Scottish variation of John. I have no idea why my mother and

father decided to have two Johns in the house, a John and an Ian. Deirdre is my sister's name but that is an old Irish name, from folklore.

Were you brought up bilingually?

No, but my Dad was a native Irish speaker. Irish would have been an academic subject in our house and he would only use Irish with someone who had excellent Irish. But it was around the house and we were accustomed to it.

What sort of childhood did you have?

We were very happy. I think that happiness came from the fact that we were very secure where we lived. We lived a country life: my father was a schoolteacher and a farmer and my mother was at home. I don't really remember when I was very small, when my mother was a hotelier. Life would have been different then. Every summer was lovely – I'm sure it wasn't – and Christmas was fantastic, although I'm sure there was the odd row. You remember whatever you want to remember. But I do remember a lot of happiness and contentment and we were protected in many ways in the life that we lived. It was very much rural Ireland and we were part of the community. My father was a big community activist and that was the life we led for many years.

Were politics in the air in your family?

Politics weren't in the air when I was very young. They became an item of discussion only when Clement, my uncle, became involved at national level. He was in the county council since the 1960s but my mother had protected us from politics completely. After Joe Brennan died [in 1980] we became involved coming up to the convention and during the entire election campaign.

Clement won the seat. We were probably a hindrance more than a help, It was only at that stage that national politics would have impacted on the family. Prior to that my father would have been involved to a lesser extent as secretary of the cumann. We would have been accustomed to him going to conventions; it was just something he did. In the 1980s life was difficult, politics were difficult and we would have heard adult conversations going on about what was happening, and the whole thing about Charlie Haughey. I will never forget the time of the budget [in 1982] when we got the phone call to say that the Coalition government had fallen. Clement had just gone through a by-election and now we were into our second election and before he died he had a third election [again in 1982], so it was a very traumatic time. There were small children at home so it was a huge imposition on people's lives. It was only at that stage that politics *per se* really got into the family.

Tell me about your own entry into politics.

When I came to Dublin to study in UCD I did the same as every other child of a TD. You came in to Leinster House on Wednesday evenings, got your tea, made a few phone calls, helped out with a few letters and hopefully met Dad to get a few quid to keep you ticking over for a week. That is how I started in the Dáil. I got involved in Ógra Fianna Fáil through the cumann in UCD. I also studied politics.

In June 1986 when Dad died I was the eldest and had just done my finals. I was asked to put my name forward for his seat. With hindsight I know that my mother was not particularly anxious that I would go into politics. I remember coming up to the Dáil with my brother Michael to clear out Dad's things. I thought I had sneaked in nice and handy but the next thing I got a call that Charlie [Haughey] was looking for me. I went up for an inquisition. I didn't know it was an inquisition at the time, but I knew it afterwards. That is how I got involved. The local cumann put pressure on me to run for the Dáil.

What happened then?

I was co-opted to the county council in October 1986 after my father's death. Fine Gael was in government at the time and Paddy Harte [Donegal TD] proposed in the Dáil that there was no need to have a by-election because there was going to be a general election. So that is what happened and my Dad's secretary was allowed to remain in the job to finish off all the work that had to be done. Then there was a convention in January 1987 and the election in February so we were straight in there in 1987.

You were very young.

I was just turned twenty-one when I went into the Dáil. I was the youngest in the House for a considerable number of years and was glad to get rid of that label. I think about what would have happened if I hadn't taken the job. I wouldn't be in national politics and I wouldn't be a minister. Life would have been totally different. Like a lot of my colleagues I might gone to the UK or somewhere else to study or to work.

Before becoming involved in politics, what did you want to do?

I wanted to do social work. I thought that I would specialise in psychiatry afterwards. My mother was a psychiatric social worker so I had an interest in that. Someone said to me many years later: 'Well sure, isn't that what you're doing anyway?' And that mightn't be far off the truth. But my first election was a daunting task. However, at the time I got caught up in the excitement of what was happening, and didn't analyse the long-term impact it would have to the same extent that I would today.

How would you feel if your twenty-one-year-old son or daughter announced that he or she was going to run for the Dáil?

I would not be encouraging it, although when you talk to other people they say there is nothing much you can do about your kids, except help them make their own decisions. A lot of us came through political families but that scenario will change. And also people won't stay as long in politics. It is not physically possible to do it. I had many challenges when I was first elected, I would have been the same age as the daughters of the guys in the House; yet I was elected and on a par with them. I can see now how it might have been difficult for constituents to come looking for help from someone like me. I was the first woman elected and I was so young. But I had great backup, great staff and a great mother. That influenced the way I started off my political life. I had mentors, and constituents approached them if they did not want to come to me. Some people might not like that to happen but that was the reality of the situation.

What was it like for a twenty-one-year-old to be in the Dáil instead of dating and going out to dances?

I tried to keep my two feet on the ground. I went back and lived with the girls I was living with when I was in college. So I had a little bit of that type of life, normality as one might call it. That was easier in Dublin than in the country because Fianna Fáil country TDs have clinics and meetings and they work until the middle of the night. Besides, there was a number of people who didn't want me in the Dáil. That was the harsh reality of it, that's politics, and they were going to make life difficult for me. It was hard to keep on course and not turn around one day and say I was going to jack it in because it was no job for me. But I just kept going.

Did you go out on dates?

Not really. It was bizarre that I met David in the Dáil through a friend of mine, a Garda. He introduced me to David, who was one of the only people who ever asked me out. I said well if someone has the neck to ask me out I should have the manners to go out with him at least and I married him two years later. You know, not too many romances start around the Dáil but this was one of them.

It is one of the issues I wonder about. Do you think men are intimidated by the fact that women have these jobs?

I think that was definitely the case twenty years ago: no two ways about it. I think things have changed; I hope they have changed. Younger people expect things to be different. More people are going to university, more younger people are out and about working and that does change things considerably. When I started in the Dáil I would have been about the only young person I knew in a good well-paid job. Everyone else who was doing well was not in Ireland; they were somewhere else. It definitely was a factor. People can be uncomfortable with who you are. Plus you are in the public eye, which prospective partners might not want to be.

What age were you when you married?

I got married very young, when I was twenty-six. Cathal, my first child, was born the day after the general election in 1997, ten years ago. He is, naturally, named after his grandad and so far he is the only boy among my mum's grandchildren. That was a tough time. I was almost nine months pregnant during the election campaign and it drove all my family and friends daft because they were afraid something would go wrong. It was when Cathal was three years old that we found out he was deaf. In the meantime David had a very serious car accident in which he lost his leg, and then on 19 May 1999, in the middle of the local elections, Maeve arrived on this earth. So I had a fairly tough time with two kids, one of them diagnosed as deaf, and my husband losing his leg. It was a traumatic time in my life, I can tell you. But I kept hammering on at the job.

How do you manage? You are one of the very few politicians called Mary who has young children.

At that time I relied on my mother a lot. David was working nights. Cathal was more or less reared in my mother's house from the first year of his life and then I got a live in-nanny. Since David went back to his job he just works during the day and I got a full-time babysitter. That's how I manage.

How do you feel about it yourself?

I had to do something very difficult – I had to let go. My mother said to me, 'Mary, if something happens in Donegal, you're too far away so you just have to trust the people you leave behind.' And that is what I had to do. It's tough, as you know, but if I had to worry about something at home there was no point in me being in Dublin trying to do my job. So I had to let go. That is the only way you can stay sane. If you try to do everything it just doesn't work.

In the 1980s, women politicians thought we could have it all – family, job, responsibilities. Do you think now that this is possible?

You have to sacrifice something and you have to decide what you are going to sacrifice. Sometimes we end up making the wrong decisions. You sacrifice your family, your life or your marriage; you sacrifice your health. So you can't have it all. There is nobody in this world who can have everything they want. You just have to get on with it and I think that is the great attribute that women have. You decide where you are going to be and what you need to do over a certain period and then you say, 'Right, I'm going to make a go for this.'

You can't always be at home to do the homework and go through all the things the children are going through, and you are going to miss some of the little milestones in their lives. But you prioritise and sometimes the politics has to give in. I distinctly remember a very funny occasion when the late Senator Paddy McGowan insisted that we would have meetings on Sunday afternoons. One day I brought Cathal and his playpen and I plonked them down in the meeting. We never had a Sunday afternoon comhairle ceanntair meeting since that day. I made my point.

My family life is very important and there is part of it I am not going to sacrifice. And part of politics is not going to be sacrificed. But at the same time you have to keep your sanity and you have to have your health. That is not to take away from the fact that there is now an appreciation of where I am coming from as a young woman and a mother of small children. I never want people to think that I can't do my job or that things have to be sacrificed. I reflect on the fact that Dad died when he was forty-eight, Clement was killed when he was only forty, so they did not get to live life. I am forty-two and I feel I am only on the first rung of the ladder. I've been through a lot of battles – with the kids and with David, when I thought he was going to die after the accident. So you just have to make these tough decisions – something has to give.

Your mother is obviously a crucial person in your life.

Very much so. First of all she taught us all to be independent because some day we could be on our own. She also encouraged my sister and me. There was equality in our house: if the byres had to be cleaned I did them as much as the boys did the hoovering. That independent streak is very much part of where we are. I would be soft in many ways when she would be cutting-edge and you have to have someone to be like that in politics. Someone has to go out and be bold and say that something is not happening or whatever the case is. You develop that attribute after a while – it's called experience.

Would you think that your political life is different from the life of a Dublin TD?

Very much so. A Dublin TD can go home in a maximum of an hour, even with the traffic we have. If I were to travel an hour I would only be at the M50 and I would still have to go home. So there are huge differences. Plus they can do their work Monday to Friday, whereas we have to spend the weekends doing things they can do during the week, like clinics and meetings and deputations.

I would imagine that twenty years ago it was a very different story.

It was totally different: now there is a greater appreciation of family life. People are working harder and everyone is under more pressure, so they have personal experience of the difficulties. There is also an appreciation that people take time out on a Sunday. Before this Sunday was a busy day: between football and all sorts of meetings. I think because society has changed there is a greater appreciation of what everyone does. It makes it slightly easier. Sunday is now a day we like to keep for ourselves.

Are you managing to do that?
Within the bounds of possibility! There are times that you just have to give them up but that's fine. The kids get dragged to GAA matches as well but that's something we would do anyway.

All of us who have been in public life know the fear and terror of elections. How do you feel about them?
You couldn't live with me coming up to an election. David just boxes it off and forgets about it and thinks I will come back to him after the election. It's an awful, awful way to live your life: to think that you could burst yourself for five years and because of one thing or another you lose your seat. I've been very lucky; I have never lost. There are others who have lost and come back and I very much admire their willpower. Even though you may be buoyed up by the excitement of it and you drive your people and they in turn are so enthusiastic, some nights in bed you think: what am I going to do if this doesn't work out. You couldn't employ a TD – their lives are so different from everyone else's. So you think: who's going to pay the mortgage? And if you did lose how could you stay at home?

All this, plus the fact that there is an inherent need to win. That is what drives us all to do well and to win. It is not just you who has to carry that but your family as well because they get concerned about you and the stress it all creates. Then the in-fighting that happens in Parties and between Parties is just horrendous. And it is not just the three weeks of the campaign, it is now starting the year before. In the past it was almost instantaneous because we had so many elections but now you have a year of preparation and the further up the ladder you go in the Party the more stress there is.

Would you consider a change in direction now?
If I weren't a minister I might: because we all like the opportunity to move on and get new experiences. Now that I am a minister I would say not at this moment because I have enough challenges here. But you often wonder what are you going to do, because you can't be at the top of your game all the time and then will it be a soft landing or a big bang? That is something that is at the back of my mind.

I always felt the fear of failure was women's weakest point, like coming back from a defeat.
I have never experienced it personally so I can't really empathise with someone who has been through it. But I have the experience of a loss of a family seat on the county council, when you feel the family has been let down and then the Party and then yourself. I know it is an awful way to think of things. We lost the County Council seat after forty years, and it was a devastating blow to us all because we had worked at it for those forty years. We have been able to pick up the pieces. But to lose your own seat is a terrible blow and then the fear of failure – you are absolutely right. It is something men will probably go and have a crack at but women find this harder and then because of that trepidation they won't take the risk. That is why we don't get more women into politics.

We have fewer women in politics than we had some years ago. Why do you think this is?

A couple of reasons. Before this money would have been a problem. Secondly, getting through a selection convention, which is still hard no matter who you are. Sitting TDs now find it even more difficult to be re-selected. Thirdly, it's the fear of failure, no two ways about it. There's the kind of woman who provokes the response: 'Who does she think she is, strutting around there? She's going to make big speeches and change the world. We'll take the shine off her.' Then you'll get another woman who you know in your heart and soul is superb but she just won't take that step no matter how much help you give her. It's very hard to get the balance right.

How about the fact that women have more interesting career choices?

They do now. There is much more going on and less public hassle. Whatever about hassle within their own job, or remuneration, you will notice that a lot of people who are quite successful don't like being in the public eye. They want to keep their family life to themselves and keep what they do in their job within the company where they are working. That is why, although some women are superb, you can't even get them on a board. It is not that they are not there; it is just that they won't do it because they don't want to be aligned to a political party and they don't want to be put up there to be knocked. We may find ourselves in a situation where it is difficult to get great young people into the House. You need them because they have to drive the agenda for the next twenty or thirty years and that is going to be tough.

Local politics have become more and more difficult as well. The county council is now nearly a full-time job and is a great breeding ground for getting people to run for national politics. You get waves: we had a wave with women; there is a wave with Fine Gael; there will be waves with Fianna Fáil. It just comes and goes. My view is that women have a massive contribution to make to public life and we just have to find ways of keeping going. It is possible, although it needs a lot of balancing and juggling. If you are single, fair enough, but if you are married the other half has to appreciate the life that you will have. Some men don't want that.

I think that is a crucial point. It may reflect the kind of men women in politics marry.

I am lucky. David said he would never stand in my way in my career but you get the odd jibe – that's just the way it is. It really is a family business and everyone belonging to you is involved in it. It's the same kind of life as for someone who was reared in a pub – up all night and people in the door in the morning. It's a train station you live in, not a home.

Quite a number of politicians came from that kind of background: the small shop in the village where public service, in whatever guise, was very much part of the background.

They did; they were used to it. But this has changed. It's not so much part of the background any longer. Many more professional people are involved. Among the new gang that has come into the House recently, a lot of them are in the professions and ferociously enthusiastic. This is great because sometimes you despair and wonder if anyone is going to take over, or what ulterior motives people might have for coming into the House. But it is great to see people who are enthusiastic and to encourage them now so that they don't lose heart.

Máire Geoghegan-Quinn

Máire, you're a Mary but a Máire. When were you born?
I was born on 5 September 1950. I was christened Mary but then because I lived in a Gaeltacht area my name became Máire.

Are any other members of your family called Mary?
I had an aunt on my mother's side and an aunt on my father's side called Mary.

Where did you come in your family?
I was the elder of two. I had just one brother and there was a gap of four years between us.

Would you have liked to be called something else?
I suppose there was a period in my life – I think when I was in my late teens and early twenties – when I felt, oh God, why did I have to be called Máire. But then, there was a kind of acceptance as time went on. All these soap operas came on television and lots of girls I taught in school were called Crystal after *Dallas* or *Dynasty* or whatever. Then I said to myself that I liked the older names. Maybe if I had been called something else…Maeve was a name I loved and I always said if I had a little girl I would call her Maeve.

Did you?

I didn't have a little girl, no. I have two boys and they both have good old Irish names. The elder is Ruairí and the younger is Cormac.

In your class at school would there have been a lot of Marys?

An awful lot of Marys. I would say that in the village where I was brought up – Carna, fifty miles west of Galway city – almost every single family had a Mary in it. Now they might have been called Maureen or Marie or Máire, but they were Marys.

You mentioned that you had two aunts. Would you have been called after them or would you have been called Máire because every family had to have a Mary?

I think it was probably my mother trying to get a name that wasn't her own name – which was Barbara – and at the same time keeping a bit of family history alive. Because she had a sister Mary and my father had a sister Mary it was decided this would be the way. In the same way, my brother was called Seán after my father, my grandfather and my great-grandfather, who were John and Seán and Johnny.

When you were growing up you were the only daughter in the family. Did you go to college?

I went to the primary school in Carna and then I went away for five years' boarding in Tourmakeady. I wanted to do medicine and my mother intervened and said, 'Medicine is six years in college and one year as an intern and I know what is going to happen: you'll meet a fellow half-way through and fall in love. You'll decide you want to get married and medicine will go by the board.' So she said, 'Why don't you do teaching – ' she was a teacher herself ' – you can use it all over the world if you want to and you will be finished in two years' training and two years' probation. And if you want to go and do medicine you can do it after that.' Of course she had a very strong influence on my life and I did exactly as she told me: I spent my two years in Carysfort, the teachers' training college in Dublin.

Where did you teach?

First of all I taught in an-all Irish school in Dublin, Scoil Bhríde in Oakley Road in Ranelagh. I taught there for almost three years. I had met John in the meantime and we were engaged and planning to get married in 1973. He had been offered a job in Galway and I took a flyer by giving in my notice three months in advance of the beginning of July, which was what you had to do in those days. When I gave in my notice my mother nearly went mad, of course. She said, 'How could you give up a job like that without already having a job?' In the meantime a new school had been built in Renmore, on the eastern side of Galway city, and they were looking for eight teachers. I put in my application and was interviewed by five priests and the bishop up over the cathedral in Galway. Thankfully I got the job. So there was no break: by the time three months' notice was up I had started my other job.

Was your father in political life?

I was a little girl when he was elected to the Dáil. He had been on the county council before that and in 1954, the year my brother was born, he was elected to the Dáil for the first time.

So you grew up in a political household.

Yes, I grew up in a very political household. Now, having said that, at that time kids were seen and not heard so, if there were adults visiting the house, we were never in that room but sent somewhere else. So, while a lot of political discussion took place when I was very young, none of it took place within earshot. When I went to boarding school in Tourmakeady, one of the things I got very involved in there was debating. In 1965 a general election came up and I happened to be at home. My father said, 'Well now, if you are so good at talking in public all around the country on behalf of the college, why don't you get out there and get up on a wall and speak for me.' I was fifteen. So I got up on the wall outside the church in Carna in my own parish, an awful place to stand in front of your own people, and asked for votes for my father. Very amateurish it seems now, but that was the beginning of my active involvement, as it were, in politics.

How old would you have been when you went out canvassing?

I didn't go out canvassing as a young child; neither Seán nor myself did. My mother did. She was steeped in politics, more so in many ways than my father was before he was elected to the council. She was from the area and my father was a kind of a blow-in: he was from Oughterard and when he married my mother, who was teaching in Carna parish at the time, he moved to Carna to live, and built a house and all that. So her involvement would have been far greater than his at the very beginning.

Did it ever occur to her to be the candidate?

No, never. This was borne out when my father died and the organisation asked her to run. She had no interest in being out there as the front person but she was wonderful at organising and being like all the spouses of TDs were in those days – the secretary at home: taking the phone calls, opening the letters, making the calls. And doing all that for nothing.

So your mum is there and you make your first political speech at fifteen and you are in secondary school at that stage. Then what happened?

Then my father was re-elected. He was returned in every election up to the time he died in January 1975, when I was twenty-four and married. We were living in Galway, where Ruairí was born in 1974. We originally lived in a bedsit, then we rented a house and in 1975 we bought a house in Renmore. Up to the time that I got married I was determined to get involved in politics. Whatever I was going to be, it was going to be in politics. But I got married then and we settled down. We had a nice home and we both had good jobs. I could walk to work every morning. I would wheel the baby to the baby-minder and collect him on the way home at 2.30. It was a lovely lifestyle. I had my long holidays and my weekends off, and I said to myself, 'This is it now, forget about politics, I have no interest in it' – even though I knew that my father would have very much wanted for me to be involved in politics.

In 1973, after Gene Fitzgerald's by-election campaign in Cork, my father had a massive heart attack and he ended up in St Vincent's Hospital in Dublin. After that he slowed down considerably for a period of time. While I was in college in Dublin I used to go into the Dáil on Wednesday afternoons, and help him with the correspondence and getting the letters and representations out. Then when I was teaching in Dublin I would go in on Tuesday evenings as well, which is how I got to know Leinster House so well. When I came home at the weekends, if he wasn't feeling well, I would do his clinic in Galway in a little pub in Eyre Street called the Hole in the Wall. As well as my mother supporting him at home, I was there for him when he was in Dublin, away from home. He got two subsequent heart attacks and he was hospitalised in Galway and died on 5 January 1975.

We had had warnings but that Christmas before he died he was in great form although he was only out of hospital. He absolutely adored my son Ruairí. He would come in the morning before I went to school and play with Ruairí in the kitchen while I got myself ready. That was his choice and every weekend he would want Ruairí to go and stay with himself and my mother and he would get down on the floor and play with him, even after his third heard attack. So it was a major shock when it happened: he just got out of bed, told my mother he wasn't feeling very well, went to the bathroom, came back and said he had a terrible pain in his chest. And he fell back on the bed and died. It was very traumatic for my mother and for my brother and myself.

At any stage along the way had you thought that, God forbid, if he died you might run for the Dáil?

Oh no, absolutely not, I had firmly made up my mind once we got married that politics were not going to be for me. And I honestly believe that but for the fact that my father died in such a tragic way I would be teaching to this day.

At that stage – mid-1970s – the women's movement had started. Would you have been interested in it? Would you have been observing it?

I would certainly have been observing it. I suppose because of the fact that I was in Galway rather than in Dublin, where a lot of the activity in the women's movement in those days was based, I was removed from it. I felt very strongly about women's rights to this extent: that when my mother got married she had no choice but to give up her job because the marriage bar was in place. One of her biggest preoccupations in life when I was growing up was that I had to have a job no matter what it was, a job I could return to if anything happened to my husband, even if I had to give up work when I got married.

This was exactly the attitude of my own mother.
Because of that I think I felt very strongly that women should have the choice to have a job, to continue working whether married or not. That was really the only practical thing about the women's movement that I felt strongly about but I wasn't active in it at all.

But you weren't hostile to it.
Not at all, no.

I remember that Betty Friedan referred to the 'click' factor, the moment of recognition. Did you feel at any stage that you were looking at things in a different way from the way you did maybe ten years before.
Looking back on it now. I don't think I felt that way about it. I used to be very supportive of some people in the movement and then I would get very irritated with others, simply because I felt that some of the concentration was on issues that had very little relevance to the women I met, say the mothers of kids who were coming to the school to me. As I said, I lived one hundred and thirty-four miles west of Dublin and the women's movement

seemed to me at that stage to be totally concentrated among a Dublin set.

Did you ever subsequently feel differently about that?

Oh, very much so. Once I got involved in politics and went along to a number of meetings of women's organisations and got to know members of the women's movement, I had a totally different perspective. I realised that *they* felt equally strongly about the issues I felt strongly about, although we could agree to disagree.

I never put myself across as a politician who was a woman first and then a politician. I was always a politician first and a woman second and I felt at the time – I think consciously – that if I could prove as a woman that a woman could do this job as well if not better than a lot of the men, this was the best practical demonstration of what the women's movement could achieve.

And did you feel you achieved that?

I do, because I think over my twenty two-years in politics there was a lot of issues. When I was made parliamentary secretary in 1977, a lot of people sort of raised their eyebrows and said, 'Oh well, the token woman,' and that Jack Lynch wanted to be remembered in history and so on. I was very lucky that I was put in with a boss who would be regarded, (as Gerry Collins said) the most difficult minister you could have – Dessie O'Malley. Now, contrary to everyone's opinion, I had an amazing working relationship with him. He gave me a job a do, which was in the commerce division of the department. He said, 'I don't want you near me unless you have a major problem that you really feel you cannot resolve on your own. Apart from that, he said, it's yours.' He brought in the department secretary and the assistant secretaries of the department and said, 'Mrs Geoghegan-Quinn is responsible for this area and I don't want anyone coming to me with problems from this area. She is the Minister for Commerce.'

How old were you at this stage?

I was twenty-six in 1977, so I had an amazing apprenticeship with him. I put in place a lot of good consumer legislation because consumer law had not been updated since the 1800s. I took the opportunity and I relished it.

My second child was born in 1979. Obviously Des O'Malley knew I was pregnant. I went home at the end of June and Cormac was born on 5 July. The Dáil closed for the summer in the middle of July. I had made a conscious decision to nurse the baby and that I was going to nurse him for six months. Now don't ask me whether I had worked out how it was going to be possible to do it and do the job as well.

That July Ireland took over the Presidency of the European Union and Des O'Malley was very busy. July and August were kind of slow on the European front but in September it started to get busy again and about the middle of September I got a phone call at home one day and it was Des himself on the phone saying, 'Hello, are you ever coming back to work?' I said, yes, but it's like this, 'I have a baby and I'm nursing the baby and I can only go back if arrangements are put in place so that I can work and feed the baby at the same time.' 'OK,' he said. 'I'll get George Colley to call you.' George Colley was Minister for Finance and the Public Service at the time. And I will never forget George Colley's phone call. He said, 'Máire, I have been talking to Des. He tells me that he needs you to come back to work and that you said you have to put something in place to be able to do this. Now, Máire, the way I look at it is that this is the first time this has happened. We have an opportunity now to set a standard that will be followed by everyone else, so let's do it properly.' And that really impressed me because here was a man who had been challenged for the first time in relation to this, and he was rising to the challenge.

He also had a very feminist wife.

He had, another Mary. I came back up to the department and there was a little office adjacent to the minister's office. They took away all the furniture and filing cabinets and rigged it up for a baby. When I was in Dublin I was staying with a friend who was a teacher in Scoil Bhríde. Her niece, as luck would have it, was doing her H.Dip in Education at the time. So she came in during the day and studied and looked after the baby and then I took the baby home with me at night. And that worked really well. Now an awful lot of people said Máire Geoghegan-Quinn breast-fed the baby in the Dáil but I never did. I breast-fed the baby in my own office or in that little office. I felt at the time that you have to be conscious of people's sensitivities and it is not something you can do everywhere and not in public.

The difficulty arose for some people when I was invited to open things and go to functions around the country. The first thing my private secretary would say when someone would ring was, 'Well now, you know the minister is nursing a baby at the moment. The baby will be coming with her so if a room could be provided where the baby can stay while the minister is doing the opening it will be possible.' I remember thinking I had really arrived when *Business and Finance*, which used to have a gossipy column on the back page, wrote about me being late doing an opening in Navan or somewhere, despite having a reputation for always being on time. Of course this was not her fault, they wrote, as the baby had to be fed and that had to come first.

So I did that until there was a change of government. Charlie Haughey became Taoiseach and I was appointed a minister. So I got almost my full six months nursing Cormac, which was great, and I felt good about it.

I would be interested in how you feel now about the family and politics. When people like me were starting out we kept insisting that it wasn't going to make any difference and that we could manage the family too. But I have been struck by the kinds of husbands the women who got themselves elected have, women like my sister Nora.

I think all the women I know, including Nora, who were interviewed during their time in politics, paid tribute to the spouse who was at home. Everyone knew who the wife of, say, Michael O'Kennedy or Charlie Haughey was, but very few knew the husbands. In my case he was John Quinn. He *wasn't* Geoghegan-Quinn and it used really to annoy me when people referred to him as Mr Geoghegan-Quinn. People, including my own family, would laugh at me because I would always introduce him as John *Quinn*, to make a point. He held down his own job and was working five days a week, sometimes six days, as a service engineer with Crown Control Forklifts,. He went on to have his own business.

At the very beginning I couldn't have survived in politics without my mother-in-law. She lived in Tuam and I would drive to Tuam on a Tuesday morning, drop Ruairí with all the paraphernalia, drive to Dublin across the bog road into Ballinasloe and so on, and on the way down on a Thursday night do the reverse and pick him up.

As time went on I realised there was no way I could continue doing this or that she could continue doing it; it was unfair. So, I found a baby-minder who lived in, Monday to Friday, in our house: and then I came home at the weekend, and between John and myself we would look after him. When we had two kids it was the same thing really.

But did I suffer from guilt? Of course I did, all the time, about all the little accidents and minor upsets that happened. I always said, even though I knew in the back of my mind it was illogical, that if I had been there it wouldn't have happened. Or I would think: why couldn't I have been there? Ruairí wrote a piece about me in the *Sunday Tribune* at one stage and he said that he always remembers he had either mumps or measles and I went off on a Tuesday morning and he cried all day because I wasn't around. Now he never told me that at the time. I am not sure if I was even aware of it because as far as I was concerned he was well cared for: he was warm, he went to school. If he was sick John was there if I wasn't there. But looking back on it years later, he remembered that particular incident.

All women who were elected at that time felt guilty about their children in one way or another but certainly I would have found it difficult to admit that in public. You had a public issue with one of your children. What was it and how did you react to that?

We were having a Fianna Fáil front-bench think-in, in Malahide, Bertie Ahern was leader of the party. I got a phone call from John at around 11 o'clock. He said there had been an incident in St Mary's College in Galway that apparently concerned Cormac. He said there was a whole group of students involved but the college was proposing to expel Cormac and three others.

He was ringing me because he knew well the journalists would pick up on it because of whose son it was. I said I would leave immediately and come home. I got into the car and drove home in a very emotional state.

When I arrived home Cormac was there and he was very upset, He said, 'You know, Mum, I wasn't involved in anything that doesn't go on in the college every single year.' Apparently it was a ritual that involved the seniors taking on the next class to them and having a battle in the dormitories. The priests all knew about, it he said, and it had also happened when Ruairí was at school there (in fact Ruairí got a very severe knee injury that we never knew about at the time). There was no priest or adult present, but four of the boys were picked out and made an example of, and he said that when the particular incident took place, he was downstairs talking to his girlfriend on the phone. So I said, 'OK, Cormac.' I took all the details and the names of the lads involved from him.

We rang the college and made an appointment to visit the President. John and I went up to the President's office with Cormac the following morning, and the Dean was there as well. I got really angry at the meeting. I wanted the answer to one question: why, in the absence of an adult witness, it was decided to pick four students out and make an example of them.

I said, 'Either you pick out the whole lot or you pick out nobody but why pick out four?' And in all the time we were there, about an hour and a half, the President could not tell me how they had come to that decision. He kept looking at the floor, which really got me angry, and eventually I said, 'I would appreciate it if you looked at me when we are talking to each other.' And I got the distinct impression that they realised they had made a mistake with all four kids but they were not going to back down. He eventually said, 'Well, of course we would like him back as a day boy. We don't want him as a boarder but we would like him back as a day boy.' And I said, 'No thank you. Every time someone does something wrong in a class or on the playing field, do you want the teachers saying, "Ah sure, that was Cormac Quinn."' I said he was not going to go through that. So he was not going back to that school. And he did not.

You faced several political issues, including the decriminalisation of homosexuality. What was the reaction of your colleagues? Was it daunting?

Yes, a number of prominent colleagues, but not members of the government or junior ministers, came to me and said it was going to be a bloodbath and they were going to eat me alive. And I said, 'OK, that's fine.'

Before I spoke to them, I met a wonderful woman, Phil Moore, whose son was gay. She had founded a support group for the parents of gay people. Her advice was invaluable.

I arrived into the parliamentary party meeting, stood up and gave my spiel about what was in the Bill. Then I put down my papers and I said, 'OK, I'm looking around the room and the vast majority of my colleagues here are men. The vast majority of you are married and a substantial number of you have teenage sons, So let me paint a picture for you – ' And I painted the picture that Phil painted for me. I said, 'Your son is nineteen, twenty, twenty-one. He comes in and tells you he is gay, And what do you do? You do the rounds, you go to the priest, the doctors and all the rest of it, and at the end of the day are you going to say to him that just because he is gay and different and practises something you don't approve of, you are going to throw him out?' Not one member of the parliamentary party asked a question. It went through. I could see as I was doing this that people were suddenly asking themselves that question: could it happen to me?

There was much the same reaction to unmarried mothers. Do you remember?

I do, yes, exactly.

So then we went to the Dáil and Fine Gael proposed this ludicrous amendment that you would have one age of consent for heterosexuality and a different age for homosexuality and I said, 'Look either you know what you are or you don't at seventeen years of age, but we are not going to go into the business of having two different ages.' And it went through.

Some people, who had said things to me before the Bill came before the Dáil, in the end didn't say anything because – as I had done at the parliamentary party meeting and as I subsequently did with all the members of right-wing Catholic groups who were on Rodney Rice and other radio programmes with me – I put every single one of those men in the position where they had a teenage son. I used sons because interestingly enough I discovered during the debate that a lot of people could handle lesbians but could not under any circumstances tolerate homosexual males. And the legislation went through the Dáil.

They were celebrating in my department because I think nobody there really believed that this was going to go through. They didn't even think it would go through the Fianna Fáil parliamentary party. [Charlie] McCreevy said to me at the time, 'The Party grew up today.' And it was true in a way because a lot of those deputies had to say, 'Well, maybe she's right.'

I went to a Fianna Fáil organisation meeting in Galway West two weeks after the legislation had gone through and before the end of the meeting I was attacked by four or five guys. Oh, God bless us, they were saying that what I had done was terrible and anti-Catholic and anti-Church and all the rest of it. I stood up and told them exactly why it had been done, and again I told them to imagine they had a son and he came through the door and so on.

I never told John what went on at the Party meeting but about a month later John was in town and he met a very good friend of ours who was involved in the Party. This man said, 'You know something, John, my wife and I prayed for Máire the other night. And John said, 'Really? Why?' And he said, 'Our son came home – he is twenty-five years of age – and he came into the kitchen and told us he was gay. I had told my wife the story that Máire told at the meeting and I said to him, 'Well you're twenty-five. We've loved you all this time. You have an alternative lifestyle that we don't approve of but you will always be our son and we'll always love you.' And this man said to John that what I had said helped them to cope.

If it happened to this man I'm sure it happened to other members of the Party at some stage, or to someone they knew.

There was no pressure from anyone; it just happened for a practical reason. I didn't want David Norris taking another case and the country getting criticised again in the European Court.

When did you leave the Dáil?

I retired from the Dáil at the 1997 election. The incident at my son's school in January of that year that I already related to you was the last straw. He was the only one who was publicly named and I believed then, and still believe, that it was because of who his mother was that this happened. I felt strongly then, and still do, that the families of politicians are not fair game for media intrusion.

Did you miss politics?

I missed the camaraderie with colleagues and the opportunities to bring about change by legislation, but definitely not the constant driving between my home and Dublin or indeed the day-to-day mundane political activity.

What did you do after you left?

I wrote a weekly column for *The Irish Times*. I jointly presented a weekly television programme on TG4 with Fine Gael's Alan Dukes. I worked as a consultant and was a member of the board of Aer Lingus.

Tell me about being offered the job in the European Court of Auditors.

At the end of August 1999 I was on holidays in Spain with my friend Senator Ann Ormonde. The Taoiseach's private secretary rang me on my mobile phone and asked me for a contact landline so the Taoiseach could ring me later that evening. When I enquired what it was all about he told me he had no idea. That evening Bertie Ahern rang. We had a general chat first and then he said he needed me to do something for him. I replied that I would be happy to help in any way I could but that I was in Spain at the time. He said he wanted me to go to Luxembourg for six years to be the Irish member of the European Court of Auditors. I said I'd have to talk to John and asked when he needed an answer. He said within the hour!

I then rang John who was playing golf in Galway Bay Golf Club. He was on the course and not very happy to have to answer the phone. I asked him if he'd come to Luxembourg for six years with me. He said, 'Of course I'd love to but now I have to get off the phone.' I rang Bertie back and within a short time I received a fax announcing my appointment.

How has your life changed since you were appointed to that job?

I love the challenge. I feel very privileged to have been given the opportunity by the Taoiseach and the government, not just once but for a second mandate. I'd never lived abroad before 2000. It's very different. Luxembourg is small and people are very reserved so its not that easy to make Luxembourgish friends. They close their shutters early in the evening; one never hears any noise.

From a language point of view I find Luxembourg fascinating – they have their own Luxembourgish language which everyone uses all the time, in shops, schools, civil service, local authorities, police force, health, public transport – every aspect of normal daily life. That's despite the fact that it's a tiny country (400,000 population) and is surrounded by Germany, France and Belgium.

Luxembourg is a country ideally located in the centre of Europe so one can drive to different places easily. Working with twenty-six different nationalities is a real challenge. We all have very different cultures so what might be a joke in the English language could be regarded as a insult in another. One needs to be careful! My colleagues come from many different backgrounds – auditing, the law, academia, public service and politics. It's a good mix and makes for lively discussions a lot of the time.

When I came to the job in 2000 French was the dominant language of the Union. But, with the accession of the ten central and eastern European countries, that has changed and now English is the dominant language.

As for me, life goes on and time marches more quickly as I get older. The most significant thing that has happened to me in recent years is that in 2005 I became a grandmother for the first time. I find it this new role incredibly exciting, rewarding and fulfilling.

Mary Hanafin

Where are you from and where do you live now?

I live in Dublin, having grown up in Tipperary. I was in school there so I suppose I would always be considered a Tipperary person. I taught in Dublin for seventeen years and I was elected in Dún Laoghaire. So if the question were posed: if Tipperary and Dublin were in an All-Ireland final, who would I support? – I am always hopeful that it will be Tipperary in the hurling and Dublin in the football and I'll get to support both!

How old are you?

I was born in June 1959.

Where do you come in your family?

The elder of two. I have a brother John who has just been re-elected to the Seanad.

Do you have any knowledge of why you were called Mary?

I was meant to be Lisa, apparently, which probably would have been an unusual name in 1959. But at the birth I gave my mother such trouble and there were so many prayers to Our Lady that I was called after the mother of God.

Since then, has the Mary name been an issue in the family or in school?

No, there were loads of Marys in my class.

How many?

About four, I think.

Out of how many?

Nobody ever took any notice of class sizes until this year so I don't know how many of us were there but it was quite a common name then so it wasn't an issue.

What is your second name?

Teresa – I am a little flower. It is only now that I notice as Minister for Education that when I go around to schools and ask the children, 'Is there any Mary in the class,' there are never any Marys. Then I say, 'Did anyone have a mammy called Mary?' and you rarely get that now. So I stopped asking the question when one child said, 'Well, my nana is called Mary.' I realised that I was ageing myself and everyone else.

Are you one of the last Marys in politics?

I don't know. It's a strong feature of Fianna Fáil in particular that we have a lot of Marys. Maybe we are more traditional in our ways. It may be the case that in politics people like to have something that they are comfortable with.

You are the second person who said that to me.

Am I? Mary is a comfortable name and I might also say a teacher is someone with whom people are comfortable. You have a large number of teachers elected as well. People like to feel that they know you and that they don't have to keep going through loads of barriers, even spelling your name. So immediately you have a more comfortable link with them.

The people you meet in your political life, as opposed to your friends, do they call you Mary?
They all call me Mary. It can't really be abbreviated.

They don't call you Miss Hanafin?
That's very interesting. If I'm canvassing and a door opens and someone says, 'Hello, Miss Hanafin,' my question instantly is, 'Whose mother are you?' because it means I taught their child. If they say, 'Hello, Minister,' I generally ask what department they work in because they are usually a civil servant. Then if they say, 'Hello, Mary,' you know you have the vote. What is interesting is that every child I meet – and I obviously have an awful lot of contact with children because of my job – will always go, 'Hello, Mary Hanafin.' You get the whole name, so you end up definitely with the Christian name which wouldn't be usual for a child talking to someone older or someone in authority, but they include a sense of respect by adding the surname.

Are you always connected with your surname to distinguish you from other Marys?
Yes, that would certainly come through, although I have been introduced on radio and at conferences – not so much now but certainly in the early days – as Mary Harney. Hers was the name that rolled off the tongue most quickly because people knew her in a position of authority. People who made the mistake got very embarrassed by it. This happened when Mary Harney was Tánaiste and I used to pass it off by saying, 'I wish I was the

Tánaiste.' It was embarrassing when it also happened once or twice on radio, but it doesn't happen as much now. The surname going with it distinguishes you from the other Marys.

You are older than your brother?
I am fifteen months older than my brother. He has a grand ordinary name, John.

Was your father in politics when you were a child?
Yes. My father was elected to the county council in the early 1950s and was chairman of Tipperary County Council when he was only twenty-four. So even before I was born he was heavily involved.

He was also a Senator. When was that?
He was elected to the Seanad in 1968, when I was nine. So I grew up in a political household.

Did you go out on the Seanad campaign with him?
My mother and I used to do part of the country, particularly the Sligo/Leitrim/Roscommon/Mayo end, which was a long way from home. My father used to concentrate on other areas.

Where was your mother from?
Clonmel, I am thoroughbred Tipperary. My father is Thurles so we have North and South Riding combined.

Is your mother political?
Oh, my mother is as much a politician as any of us. She canvassed for John this time.

With him or separately?

Separately. She did Wexford because my father was in hospital in Waterford at the time so, rather than just be visiting and doing nothing, she canvassed. So it was very much a political household. Between my mother and her link with Padre Pio and my father and politics – and then my aunt Binky Hanafin, my father's sister, became a councillor and chairman of the county council in North Tipperary – politics wasn't just on the male side.

When would you have decided that you might be interested in politics?

I spoke at my first Ógra Fianna Fáil youth conference shortly after I did my Inter Cert. I still have the photograph that appeared in, I think, the *Irish Press* at the time. The first three speakers were Michael Hanna, who is now a High Court Judge, Mary Harney and myself. I was very young but I was hugely impressed by these Trinity students, as they were at the time. I remember particularly one fellow with beautiful Irish because I always loved the Irish language. So I was very vocal from a very early stage. I boarded in the Presentation in Thurles for the last three years of school because Daddy was the fundraiser for the Party at the time. He was spending a lot more time away from Thurles but we did not want to move out of the town. The sister in charge, Sister Alice, used to let me go out to cumann meetings in the town.

She was obviously a Fianna Fáil supporter.

She probably was, God rest her: she died a couple of years ago. But the idea of letting a young student out! The meetings used to take place in Hayes's. I think she thought they took place in

Hayes's Hotel, but in fact they took place in Hayes's the Arch Bar. I'm not sure she knew she was sending me out to a pub every month.

At what stage in your life did you want to be a candidate and did your father support you in this?

I went to college in Maynooth and set up the first Fianna Fáil cumann there. I had to get special permission to set it up and in fact Tomás Ó Fiaich, who was President at the time, sent for me to congratulate me on doing it. Fine Gael and Labour immediately followed. Our cumann got quite active doing research and polling and bringing in guest speakers. Then I was elected as a youth member of the Fianna Fáil national executive in 1980 and I have more or less been a member of the national executive since then, holding many different positions, as a youth member, then as a member of the Committee of Fifteen, which is elected by the Ard Fheis – this is the committee everyone considers all-powerful. Then I was treasurer of the Party and then a front-bench member, so I came up that way.

As regards running as a candidate, Joe Little said to me recently that he met my father in Thurles in the 1980s and my father told him that I was interested in running as a candidate but there was no way he was going to be letting me out on the highways and byways of the countryside late at night, and if I was going to run it was not going to be in Tipperary. I had never heard this. I think he felt it was very difficult for a TD from the country and particularly for a woman in the country. Dublin was where I set my sights.

At that stage you were teaching in Sion Hill.

Yes, Sion Hill in Blackrock, teaching Irish and History. That was from 1981.

Where did you meet your late husband?

I met Eamon through Ógra Fianna Fáil, in fact, through the meetings that we used to go to in UCD. Then we used to meet up at various conferences, so that was the link.

What age were you when you met him?

I met Eamon in 1980 so I was 21.

When were you married?

In 1985.

While he wasn't in elected politics he would have been supportive?

Oh hugely supportive, not even just as a support to me but an active participant in policy-making, speech writing, in direction. Very much the man behind the woman.

Did you ever fancy anyone from another political Party?

No, my whole circle was always Fianna Fáil. It would have been very difficult for someone from another party. I don't know how difficult it would have been for me but it would have been very difficult for them.

So you were married for twenty years.

Married in 1985 and Eamon died in 2003. Eighteen years.

It was a very sad time for you I have no doubt, a horrible shock.

Well you can't really explain to anyone what a sudden death is like. Only someone who has experienced it themselves can appreciate it.

You were away when it happened?

I was going to a United Nations conference in Peru and Eamon was at the Morris Tribunal in Donegal. He was representing the Gardaí there. It was a very lovely bright sunny morning, a Tuesday, and we sat outside at the back of the house and had our breakfast before he went. For some reason, when I went into the kitchen, I saw the camera sitting on the table, one of these disposable cameras, and I went out and I took his photograph. He asked, 'What are you doing that for. Are you trying to finish the film'?' I wasn't even trying to finish the film, and I said no.

When were you first elected to the Dáil?

In 1985 I was proposed and seconded for the local Dublin Corporation election at the convention in Rathmines. I got no votes at all which meant that everyone was proven to be a liar because even if there had been one vote for me they could all claim that it was theirs. I was added to the ticket and elected and then in 1989 I wanted to run for the Dáil in that same constituency, Dublin South East. Charlie Haughey, to his credit, wanted me to run in Dún Laoghaire, but I knew it all. I said I was on the council in the Rathmines ward but he said that the fact that I was teaching in Dún Laoghaire meant that would be a the better base for me. Of course he was right and I was wrong. I ran in Dublin South East and didn't get elected. Eoin Ryan, who was also a candidate, was appointed to the Seanad after that election as one of the Taoiseach's eleven and this gave him the more solid base for the future.

Who was the Fianna Fáil TD at the time?

Ger Brady was the TD. Then in 1991 even though my vote went up from 800-plus to nearly 1200, I lost my seat on Dublin Corporation. I think it was because I was the second Fianna Fáil seat and Michael Donnelly was the Lord Mayor at the time. I did not know where I was going or what I was going to do politically so over the next two years I did the legal studies diploma in DIT in the evenings to occupy the time and energy that I had been giving to the Corporation prior to that. Teaching was my full-time job between 1981 and 1993.

Then in 1993 I was at a Fianna Fáil national executive meeting and they were talking about restructuring the executive, limiting the time for some members but not for senior positions. So I decided to contest the position of treasurer of Fianna Fáil at the Ard Fheis, which was unheard of at the time. For the first time in years I forced an election, pushing the incumbents, who included Bertie Ahern, to the poll. I toured the country, got huge support and was elected joint treasurer of Fianna Fáil with Bertie Ahern. It was this that started me on the political road again. I remember sitting in the Berkeley Court that December having tea with Bertie and him saying to me that where I needed to be was in Dún Laoghaire. He said I should join a cumann there, get involved and run.

And who was the Fianna Fáil person there?

It was David Andrews forever, and then you had Brian Hillery who had lost his seat and Betty Coffey, who had been a great stalwart as a councillor over the years but had never managed to be elected to the Dáil. Martin O'Donoghue had come and gone. Fine Gael was rock-solid with very strong personalities – people like Seán Barrett and Monica Barnes. Eamon Gilmore of Labour was there, another very strong person. So I took Bertie's advice, which was the same advice Charlie Haughey had given me. At least I gave myself a better run-in on it this time. I went for a convention there in 1997, didn't get through that convention either but was added to the ticket and elected that year. I was returned in the two subsequent elections.

That election in 1997 was in the summer. I remember it because it was the year I ran for President.

That election was in June, which suited me perfectly because it came at the end of the academic year. I started campaigning the year before. I was a full year out knocking on doors and I had a great team of women with me.

David Andrews was still there so we won a second seat. Niamh Breathnach was the outgoing Minister for Education and she lost her seat. It was a result that got a lot of attention at the time because no one knew who this teacher was who suddenly came along. I had built up a good base over the years with the school.

Do you mind if I ask you how you feel about women in politics with children and families?

I really don't know how they manage because it is such a demanding lifestyle. It is probably – dare I say it – easier for the TD from Dublin than it is for someone from a country constituency but even at that you don't have many women TDs in Dublin with a family. At least in Dublin you get home very night.

Would you think you would have gone into politics if you had children?

Yes, I probably would because it was in my blood. But I think it is particularly difficult for people who have to travel. If you have to come from Donegal or anywhere far away it is really very difficult and this has to be one of the biggest factors militating against women going into politics.

Clearly at the beginning of the women's movement, we were very reluctant to accept this. You had to keep pretending it wasn't that hard, although it was. That is why I didn't run until my daughter was fifteen.

I don't mean to be critical of anyone but I am not sure that at the time those women's organisations really took into account families rather than just women. I was never involved in women's political associations. While other women were involved in those groups I was still involved in youth work, so I went directly from being young to being a TD and bypassed the whole women's organisation thing. For some time women felt they had to go it alone in politics and it is only more recently that people are beginning to realise that this involves a wider family effort and a wider community effort, no matter what you are trying to do. If you look at the education statistics, the vast majority of teachers are women but the principals are mostly men. Most of the people qualifying in the top professions now are female, yet in academic life and elsewhere it is still predominantly male at the top levels. So we have to accept there is more to it than just being able and confident and having the drive to do it. You need the support structure around you.

I have always been struck by the kinds of husbands women who went into politics had in those years. For instance, my sister Nora: her husband, Brian, was great with the kids. Could they have done it without the kinds of husbands they had?

I can't comment in relation to a particular family situation. Just talking for myself, politics is a very public life even if you are a backbench TD. You appear on television, in newspapers; there are comments about you. Then when you become a minister, you are not only recognised on the street – you are public property. That puts huge pressure on other people around you. I called into a shoe shop in Ballina during the Seanad campaign and the owner said to me, 'I saw the lovely shoes you wore at the INTO conference.' And that is a shoe shop I was never in before in Ballina! Obviously the politicians themselves learn to cope with that but your family has to cope with it as well. And that can be very tough.

I have noticed, not just in Ireland but internationally, that the families of politicians sometimes pay a high price.

I think you either love it or hate it. It's one extreme or the other. You follow the path as I have done or you reject it completely. But I think also that the partner has to be confident and comfortable in their own profession. I was lucky that Eamon was a senior person who was well recognised and who had achieved high status in the Bar, so there was never any kind of competition. But it must be difficult for a partner who is not that comfortable in themselves to feel that they are being surpassed all the time.

Mary Harney

Where did you come in your family?
I was the eldest of five children, three boys in the middle between two girls.

Your parents lived on until what age?
My father died when he was eighty-three, six years ago, and my mother died just this summer and she was eighty-four.

So you would have known your parents well?
Very well, yes.

And would you have been the responsible oldest child?
Yes, but I don't know whether that was because of being the eldest or a combination of personality and being the eldest. But yes, I would have been an adult when I was still a child. For example I remember when I was about nine helping my mother with Santa presents for my two brothers, which I thought was fantastic because there was no Santa and I was in on the big secret. I think this happened to me at a younger age than my peers in general at the time and perhaps it came from being the eldest or a combination of being the eldest and being quite nosy and finding things out and discovering toys and things.

Did you come from a political family?

Only in the sense that my parents were very interested in current affairs and my father was an activist for Fianna Fáil. But obviously they weren't career politicians or anything like that. And in fact when I was growing up the idea that someone like me could become a politician was unheard of. Generally, as a female in particular, you either had to be the daughter of or perhaps the granddaughter or the widow of the male TD.

In my early years in politics, most of the women in the Dáil were connected to the previous holders of the office who were men. Eileen Lemass and Síle de Valera came from a strongly political family, Joan Burke and Celia Lynch succeeded their husbands, but many of them were suddenly thrown into the situation because they had been widowed and then won the by-election. In those days, although not so much now, it was a real partnership: the wife was the receptionist, answering the telephone, answering the door when people called at all kinds of hours. I think it is much more structured now and that does not happen. I think people are better organised because they have clinic times and lots of staff.

When I came into the Oireachtas first, senators shared a secretary with three TDs. You gave the secretary your tape and took your place in the queue. If you were from Dublin you had Monday or Friday and the rural people had access on Tuesday, Wednesday and Thursday. Nowadays I think people structure their lives a bit better. That is not to say that we don't put in the same kind of hours and maybe in rural constituencies people still call to the TD's house, but they don't in urban areas.

Would you think that it is mainly the wives who are still taking care of the children?

Oh yes. Women who are in politics worry more about their children than men in politics do. I rarely hear a male colleague worry that he is not going to see his kids at nights or at weekends but I do hear the women speak about it all the time.

Not many women in politics have children.

No...well, Liz O'Donnell did in our party and more recently Mary Coughlan has young children and she is from Donegal.

When we were heading out in the 1970s and early 1980s we didn't want to admit that it was hard or that we weren't able to have it all, so to speak. But I notice that a lot more of my generation is admitting now that it is very difficult to have it all.

Well it is. I think to juggle the children and the family and the professional piece when you are in any kind of job is difficult. But it is particularly so in politics where you work evenings and weekends and it is not a nine-to-five job, it is not predictable. If there is a local meeting about a big issue, you have to be there. You have to be in Dublin, you have to be at home if you are not from Dublin, and it is particularly difficult if you are not from Dublin.

I was nominated to the Seanad in my early twenties. I was in Trinity and I was interested in politics. Out of the blue I was appointed to the Seanad by Jack Lynch because they were looking for young people and women, although I thought my career was destined to be accountancy. I wonder now if I would have stuck with accountancy. Because politics intervened at that point I made huge sacrifices family-wise. When my friends were going to discos or dances or whatever I was going to cumann meetings or residents' meetings. I remember a friend of mine saying in about 1979-80, when I was trying to get elected – probably just before the 1979 local elections – that I was crazy, that I never came out any more. I sacrificed a lot in those years for my career; they were the years when you tend to meet people, get married and settle down.

If marriage had come first and I had been lucky enough to have children, I don't know whether I would have chosen politics or family. I think it is much easier if you are in another career where you can be half-time or take time out. You can't do that in politics: you can't take time out; you can't take a career break; you can't take a sabbatical; you can't go on half-time. You *can* go on half-time but you won't be elected again. And, because there are so few women, they are more noticed in their absence than men.

They are also more noticed for good things. I was at a Cabinet sub-committee meeting on climate change and there was a photo-call with about eight men and myself. In that situation a woman gets more noticed but equally people notice more if you are not diligent or missing meetings. And I think it is incredibly difficult to combine a career and a family. Any woman I know who does manage it, not just in politics, tends to have a very supportive family structure.

A particular kind of husband?

Yes, but also a wider family, perhaps mother, parents, maybe a supportive sister. I think the big issue for families now is the care of older people. It is becoming an issue like the care of children was in the past because there are many families where parents are in need of support.

What did your father do?

My father was a farmer.

And your mother worked on the farm?

Yes, my mother worked on the farm. My mother was very much the boss in our house; that's the way I saw it. She made what appeared to be the big decisions. My father rarely drove, for example – she did all the driving.

What sort of farmer was he?

Dairy. It was a very small farm and my father supplemented the farm income by working in a factory for many years when I was a child. He used to cycle to the meat factory in Leixlip a few days a week, which must have been very tough. Although our circumstances would not have been well off, I was not never conscious of that. It was only when I became an adult that I said, God, things must have been really difficult.

Did any other member of your family go into farming?

My brother works the farm still. It would not sustain more than one family member.

When you went to Trinity, presumably you would have been the first of your family in university?

I was the first of my family and the first of all the nieces and nephews. Most of them were younger than me. My father came from a family of five boys and three girls and they all emigrated to Chicago except for one brother. My father was destined to go there but he met my mother. My mother's family all went to Manchester. So my relatives and cousins were all living in either Manchester or Chicago and they would visit for maybe a week or two. I remember my aunt gave me £50 in 1972 when I was going to Trinity and it seemed like a huge amount of money. I worked in Chicago every summer during my college years to maintain myself in college. I got a county council scholarship to pay the fees and for pocket money I worked in Chicago. I brought home £500 in 1972, which was a lot of money.

Did your family enjoy your political life?

When I was growing up my mother encouraged me to be a teacher. She used to say if you were a teacher it was a permanent job, you finished early, you would be at home for your husband and your children. She thought being a teacher was the bee's knees; she thought you could combine having a family and children with having a steady pensionable job and if you couldn't become a teacher she used to place a very heavy emphasis on the civil service or the bank. These were seen as the big jobs. A job for life with a pension was seen as a big thing in Ireland thirty years ago.

When I rang to tell her that Jack Lynch had phoned me and that I was going into the Seanad, she was pleased but deep down I think she would have preferred if I had got married younger. I think she would maybe have preferred if I hadn't had such hassle, because in my early years of politics in Fianna Fáil I was constantly in controversy of one kind or another with the leadership. So she used to see the toll that took: the phone calls, the threatening letters, the awful side of it. But years earlier, when we were growing up, Seán Walsh, who was a TD, and Kevin Boland, who was a minister, used to call to our house from time to time because my father was an activist. Brian Lenihan too. These were big occasions: my mother and father always had huge respect for politics and did take pride in it.

Were they upset at the sort of pressure you were under?

Yes. My mother in particular would show it. She would be angry. My father didn't show it but I think he felt it and particularly all the motions of no confidence in the constituency and that side of it they found very stressful. I think they were just surprised by it, how vicious and nasty it could be. They were among my best canvassers, particularly my mother: she would canvass day and night. She loved it and she loved meeting and talking to people.

How did you feel about all that viciousness?

I could say it never bothered me but I know I am talking with hindsight. Clearly you don't like it, you don't enjoy it, but I felt very strongly about the issues at the time and I felt that the Fianna Fáil party changed when the leadership changed in 1979. It was as if I was in a different party; I felt an alien within it. The whole culture of the party changed when certain people came to the top. The people I respected were isolated, people like Des O'Malley, George Colley.

In addition, the party was adopting a very conservative approach to many of the social issues I felt strongly about. That is why, in 1985, I had made up my mind that when the next issue arose I was just not going to take it any more. It was a decision whether to stay in politics or not, to be honest with you. I had gone to America for two months with the State Department and spent a month travelling around and I did a lot of thinking on my own which is always the best thing to do and I made up my mind. The next issue happened to be the Anglo-Irish Agreement. It could have been something else but it happened to be the Anglo-Irish Agreement, and I have never had regrets about taking a stand.

You showed extraordinary courage, particularly for a young woman in the Ireland of the time. Where do you think that courage came from?

Probably from my background. My parents would have been very strong on being truthful, not that they were holier than thou or anything. It probably came a bit from that and a bit from the confidence you get from a college education I suppose, and the sense that you just didn't have to put up with this. At school I remember the girls were all protesting about something quite petty and when Sister Paula came into the class she said, 'Mary Harney, I want to see you,' and I was kind of blamed.

Why do you think you were called Mary?

Oh, it was religious. There is no doubt about that; my mother always said that. In fact my brothers all have Mary as their second or third name, such as Michael Christopher Mary. It was seen as lucky. My second brother is called after my father and my elder brother is called after his grandfather and Geraldine is called after her grandmother but for some reason Mammy didn't call either of her daughters Sarah, which is her own name. But Mary – definitely, the Blessed Virgin, you can't go wrong.

Mary Upton made the comment, 'They don't make Marys any more,' but the women I interviewed all say that people feel easy with someone called Mary.

Well, if I ever hear that someone is called Mary, I generally believe they are forty or very close to forty, certainly over thirty. I have never met a Mary whom I would regard as a bullshitter or a toffee-nose. It seems like a very ordinary name and doesn't conjure up the poshness that other names do. But I think it varies: all Marys are not the same.

Say you are out and about, not necessarily being a minister, do people call you Mary?
Yes.

They don't say Ms Harney?
Never, although sometimes a very senior person would not use your first name. For example when I was away on holiday, I was in a lovely furniture shop and a man came by, the first Irish person I had met while on holiday, and he said, 'Good Afternoon Minister,' and I said, 'Oh please…Mary,' because I hate formality. But generally people call you Mary, if it's not something worse. They feel they can call you Mary, I think.

Would you agree that there is a certain amount of ease with an old-fashioned name? I'd I say it is a generational thing.
Yes, I think it is generational. Maybe, being called something as ordinary as Mary, you don't get any notions about yourself, maybe you keep your feet more on the ground. You see very fancy names now. People have enough names for two people: double-barrel first names, double-barrel surnames. I think that conjures up an image and an air about the person that maybe keeps them somewhat removed. I think in politics people can empathise with a name like Mary. You don't sound like a person above your station, whereas if you have a very swanky name people begin to knock you straight away.

It can't be purely generational that so many politicians are called Mary or Máire.
Mary Coughlan is ten years younger than me. I am fifty-three. Mary McAleese and Mary Robinson are older than me but I don't see anyone coming up below the age of thirty called Mary.

It would be interesting to look at the registry of births.

In what sense would you feel that the political life of women has evolved in your time in politics?

I don't think women have made the strides that we sometimes assume they have made. There are still relatively few women in the Oireachtas. I feel that we still live in an environment where people think that if they have one woman or two women they have covered the women. There was a lot of progress made in the 1980s, the kind of women who came into politics as much as the numbers. Garret FitzGerald deserves a lot of credit because he brought a lot of new women into politics, not just in Fine Gael. He encouraged them. I think that progress has fallen off and there are reasons for that. Women are pursuing careers in medicine and the law and business and making different choices and I suppose political causes don't seem as strong as they used to be. A lot of women were attracted by the social agenda. People don't see the need for that any longer and the huge invasion of privacy is something they are just not prepared to put up with. It is pretty awful as you know.

Would the invasion of privacy have been as bad when you first went into politics?

Certainly not as noticeable. For example you would never be doorstepped at your house, which has happened to me in recent years. I don't remember anyone ever coming unless by arrangement. First of all we have more media, with the independent broadcasting sector, and we have a lot more media outlets than we ever had, so it is much more competitive. So from the time you get up in the morning you can look forward to being doorstepped if you have public engagements. It is no longer the case that the Taoiseach will give an exclusive interview to the *News at One* every couple of months. Now every day someone at that level can be doorstepped and interviewed.

Do you think it's unfair?

I think that it is par for the course. That is not the aspect I would complain about at all. I would complain about the invasion of privacy where the children of people in public life are under scrutiny and if their marriage breaks down it is reported in the media. That never happened before: there was always a sort of barrier beyond which the media did not go. It wasn't like the English tabloid press. There was a respect for the family and even if there was a known difficulty it wouldn't be written about. That is gone now. And with all those social columns you feel you can't go anywhere without it being written up. Standards have deteriorated, unfortunately. I think this will keep people away from politics because, although they won't mind working very hard, they won't want their whole life out in the public domain; they'll want to feel they can have a private life. Not that anyone is doing anything wrong. A lot of very successful people don't court publicity. They just want to get on with it and live their lives as best they can.

How does your husband Brian handle it?

He's got used to it, I suppose, but he doesn't like it. When we met first there used to be awful stuff because he had been married before. I was sensitive and he was particularly sensitive to what his children felt about this. So a lot of that puts people off politics. It is becoming very difficult to get certain people even to take an interest in becoming what I would call a career politician. Even when it comes to putting people on boards: if the people think it is going to attract any kind of attention, up in lights, they don't want it. They say they will do anything for me but they don't want publicity, they don't want to be in the papers. I think some people don't understand that there are other people who just like to lead private lives.

One of the things that has happened in Ireland is that people have hugely lucrative careers. Nowadays there are great opportunities in law, medicine, in accounting and business. There is a huge variety of jobs where you can make a very handsome living and people are earning a couple of hundred thousand a year. It is easy to see why people like that are not going to opt to take a huge salary cut. They can go about their business and do their work and, as someone said to me, they can play their golf on Saturday and nobody is going to worry about that.

Could you see yourself deciding not to run again?

When I came into Leinster House I used to say, I am getting out of here by the time I am forty. Now I am in my fifties and I will be nearly sixty by the time of the next election. I have always said I would like to do something else. I change my mind about what it would be. I would love to have done the Bar years ago but it just wasn't an option at the time, I should have done it when I was in the Seanad. I would like some day to go into a business or start a business. I couldn't see myself doing this forever. You can't.

Mary Henry

You are the first Mary I have met who is a Protestant. For many of the Marys the assumption was that they were called after the Virgin Mary. Why were you called Mary?

I always find this extraordinary with Roman Catholics, because the Blessed Virgin is very important in the Anglican Church. While Mary was a family name I had always assumed that the name of the Blessed Virgin was important in my naming. My mother was a member of the Mother's Union, which is an Anglican organisation for women with children – in those days I think it was married women with children – and she had the framed membership scroll. It was a painting of the Blessed Virgin by some Spanish painter. Myself, I have a great devotion to the *Magnificat*. The Blessed Virgin was quite a socialist: 'He hath put down the mighty from their seat, and hath exalted the humble and meek.'

So it is a mistake on the part of Roman Catholics to think that the Blessed Virgin is not important to members of other Christian Churches. She is important in the Orthodox Church as well. If you look at the Russian icons, she doesn't have this Renaissance pinky-white face and golden curls; she is the dark-skinned woman that she would have been. And she is given importance even in the Muslim books. I always like the section in the *Koran* where after she had given birth to Jesus she came out and sat under a date-palm tree and there was nice ripe fruit that fell down for her to eat. After giving birth they wouldn't have been too bad at all.

Where did you grow up?

In Blackrock in County Cork. I was born in 1940 and at that stage Blackrock was a very small village, only three miles from Cork city. Because I was born at the beginning of the war, walking was the mode of transport for most of the time and bikes for the rest of the time. It was a poor village, very poor indeed. We lived in what had been the gardener's cottage of a big house but in a lovely large orchard and my parents had added on to the house so that it was very comfortable.

Next door to us lived the Murphys of Murphy's Brewery. They were a very nice couple. Mabel Murphy was the sister-in-law of Terence MacSwiney. They were childless so we had the run of their enormous garden. They had greenhouses with peaches, which I can tell you was a very exotic fruit to have as a small child. They had a car. Later on in the war my father got a car too because he worked for Fry Cadbury and he had to cover quite a large area, but the car was used for business only. Apart from giving lifts to neighbours. People used to queue up at the gate to try and get a lift with him because it was a long way to get into town. I remember the morning a woman arrived with a turkey that she wanted to take to the cock to have it mated. I think was one of the most unusual passengers he ever had in his car.

Did you have Catholic friends?

We did. There was quite a separation still because Roman Catholics could not come into Protestant churches even for funerals or weddings but we could go into Catholic churches. We did have friends: the Murphys who, as I said, lived on one side of us and there were people called Quill on the other side of us but they moved shortly afterwards. Then the O'Connells moved in. He was a surgeon. He and his wife Madeleine were very good friends of my parents. The Bruens were around the corner. Then the Dunnes of Dunnes Stores fame bought the Murphys' place when the Murphys died and they were friends as well. Of course schools were much more segregated in those days. There were quite a few Jewish children in Cork then and they mainly went to Protestant schools so there were Jewish children at school with us.

Would there have been other Protestant Marys in your childhood?

There would have been but not that many.

Was it considered an unusual name then?

No, you really could not say that being called Mary would have been considered odd, not at all. I think the misunderstanding is because the Anglican Church and all the Christian Churches believe in the Virgin birth but not in the Immaculate Conception. I think there are a fair few Catholics who are a bit shaky about the Immaculate Conception as well. It is a very recent dogma, only about 150 years old.

Where did you come in the family?

I was the first.

Tell me about the kind of social world you grew up in.

For a start-off one thing that was different about us was that my father was very interested in horses and we had ponies. We had space for the ponies in the large orchard and spent an enormous amount of time with them. We were devoted to them and I can remember their names to this day. I think my mother thought it good that we were in a perpetual state of exhaustion so we could not get into trouble. If we weren't grooming them or feeding and watering them we were riding them and trying to make jumps for them. You could ride out on the roads there and along the old railway line that used to go from Cork to Crosshaven and Carrigaline. So one pony could give a lot of fun to several people because you could get on and off the ponies and bring the bikes and take turns.

Bessborough was a big convent where single mothers were sent. To this day I can remember seeing very pregnant girls in the fields pulling mangles and turnips out of the ground on cold November days. I hope the conditions weren't as harsh as they looked to me. Even to a ten- or twelve-year-old, it looked as if it was a pretty tough situation.

How would you as a young Protestant child have viewed the Catholic world where this was going on?

You must realise that it was a very small village. My mother and Mrs Murphy and a lady called Mrs Ebrill and Mother Cecilia from the Ursuline convent used to run penny lunches for the children in the Catholic primary school. So if my mother was not there when we got in from school we always knew she was at the penny lunches. There was not the strong religious separation you might expect. I remember Mother Cecilia well; she was a lovely woman.

Did you think Catholics were different? We certainly thought Protestants were different.

Not nearly as different as you did. I knew too many Catholics to think that there was some incredible difference. One thing we thought odd was that Catholics seemed to be discouraged from reading the Bible, while Bible-reading was always considered very important to us. The Latin Mass would have been different and the fact that men and women walked to church separately. There were retreats in the church and the men always went on a different night from the women. Men and women sat on different sides in the church, not as families. We always sat as families. Maybe it only happened in the country and Blackrock would have been like the country then.

What were the names of your brothers and sisters?

Robert and Joyce, which were family names. Apparently this custom has totally gone and it is going to make genealogy much more difficult. In the past if you couldn't get a link with a surname, because it was a very common surname, you looked at the Christian names. I think it was quite a good idea to use family names, rather nice.

Someone said there was a tradition of calling the first girl after the paternal grandmother.

Well, Frances is my third name, which would have been after my father's mother.

Where did you go to school?

First of all I went to Saint Michael's Church of Ireland National School in Blackrock. I was sent there when I was three to keep a second teacher in the school. This sort of thing used to happen because you had to have numbers. I think it probably happens to this day. I had an a great deal of illness as a child, and as a result of this I missed a lot of school.

I am always very enthusiastic about MMR vaccination. I was one of those people who got a measles mastoid, an infection in the bone behind the ear following measles. I constantly got infections in my ear. I missed a lot of school but I learned to read very early: I could probably read when I was four or five. And I would read everything. My mother was not that much into buying children's books so I used to read things like Edgar Allan Poe's short stories, which were entirely unsuitable for small children. Also Dickens. The print was very small in Dickens and he was very depressing because he was emphasising social problems. An aunt of mine in Dublin used to send me children's books, *The Bobtailed Pup* and that sort of thing. She was wonderful.

So you had a good family network.

We did indeed. We had my grandmother who lived in Montenotte, and I had a very dear aunt and uncle living in Douglas. My father's family were further away: one sibling was in Dublin, another in Sligo. Three of his brothers had been in the First World War. They were in a cavalry regiment and they all survived. I don't think people understand that it was the infantry that suffered so desperately. They were farmer's sons from Sligo. They turned up with their own horses in Dublin and one of them was only fourteen. He was my godfather, Andy Henry, and he was a very nice man. He lived in Dublin. I remember saying to him, 'You were only fourteen and you were able to join up?' He replied, 'A fine big fellow turning up with his own hunter. What do you think – they grabbed me at once.'

When he was sixteen his age was discovered when he was

Mary Banotti, former MEP

Mary Coughlan,
Minister for Agriculture,
Fisheries and Food

Máire Geoghegan-Quinn,
Member of the European
Court of Auditors

Mary Hanafin,
Minister for Education and Science

Mary Henry,
former Independent Senator

Máire Hoctor,
Minister of State
for Older People

President
Mary McAleese

Mary Lou McDonald, MEP

Mary O'Rourke, TD

Mary Robinson, former President

Mary Upton, TD

Mary Wallace,
Minister of State
for Forestry

Mary White, TD

Mary Harney, Minister for Health and Children

leading a charge. Whoever was supposed to be leading fell off his horse, and to his great delight Andy led the charge. Afterwards when he was called in to be congratulated, the general said, 'Private Henry, I presume,' to which Andy replied, 'No sir, Trooper Henry.' The general asked him what age he was. At this stage Andy decided to give his real age because it was legal to join up at sixteen. The general replied, 'And you have been two years in the army?'

Some people who had served in the First World War experienced criticism – that happened all over Ireland. This has totally changed now, which I think is great. I remember when the dead of all the wars began to be commemorated in Saint Patrick's Cathedral, which was a very positive thing.

Do you remember when you were growing up in Cork in the 1940s if there was a reluctance for anyone to admit that they had served in the British Army?

I would not like to say that I can personally remember it but it was certainly considered a problem. A cousin of my mother, who lived in north Cork, was home on leave from the British army. Again it was the cavalry, because they were all country boys. The IRA was pretty militant in north Cork at the time. They came to the house and said he was to be shot. But one of the girls who worked in the house ran off at considerable speed across the fields to the commandant of the IRA, who came at once and said that he certainly was not to be shot and whoever these people were, they were to get out of it. I think in general my relatives had very good relationships with other people in the area. They weren't landed gentry; they were ordinary farming people. I always remember that story and I remember the woman who, as a girl, was supposed to have run to get the commandant.

Did your parents ever talk about the Civil War?

My father's aunts, who lived in Sligo, were friends of the Gore-Booths. On of my aunts told me that Isobel was in the IRA but apparently she was only a supporter of blowing up bridges. She wasn't in favour of shooting people. My aunt said she left when that started. Her name was Isobel Fraser. I have often thought I should try and find out a bit more about her. The Rowlettes and the Frasers were friends of the Gore-Booths. They were all farmers in the area. I think Constance and her sister recruited quite a lot of young women. I don't remember any involvement in my mother's family but they would have been supporters of the new state, very much so.

Who would they have voted for?

They would probably have voted Labour.

That was quite an unusual thing.

They were very keen on social progress. They felt the country was badly held back in social issues. They would have felt that with the Catholic Church, people were not given enough information. People were very poor and there didn't seem to be a huge effort made to improve their situation.

But I remember the hymn 'All Things Bright and Beautiful', which was sung in Protestant churches, had the lines,

> The rich man in his castle the poor man at his gate,
> God made them high and lowly, he ordered their estate.

That was very much the attitude at that time. The local Catholic curate used to come see my mother sometimes to talk to her. He was in despair because he was the only one dealing with the local people's problems.

Did your mother work outside the home?

No, not after she was married. Before she was married she used to work in a very elegant dress shop called Dowdens, which was very near the Savoy cinema where Bob Geldof's mother worked. She was a friend of my mother.

Dowdens had beautiful clothes. One of my aunts was the secretary there. We sometimes went into the shop to see my aunt and we were so proud of her coming down the stairs that we nearly felt we owned part of the place.

So there you were growing up in Cork, middle-class Cork. What was the assumption about what you would do with your life?

Well, I went to Rochelle secondary school. It was a very good all-round school. Neither of my parents had had a university education, which was not that unusual in those days, although both of them were very intelligent. We were all pretty good at maths, I think because my father could work out any mathematical problem on the back of a cigarette pack. I was so often in hospital I decided to do medicine. Rochelle did not do much in the way of science and there was no Latin. Latin was obligatory to get into medicine. So I went to Alexandra College for the last two years as a boarder. Luckily I got scholarships.

So right from the start you were a very bright little girl?

That's a nice way of putting it, thank you. Scholarships were important as we weren't well off and there were three of us. I got scholarships from the time I was eleven.

Who would have told you about these scholarships?

My mother. If I could get them it was important that I did. I remember the first one I sat. We went to lunch with another girl and her mother in the Savoy cinema in Cork. This other girl and her mother looked through the papers and they agreed that they were really very simple. I said to my mother that I thought they were absolutely dreadful. But it was quite interesting because I was the one who got the scholarship.

Who gave these scholarships?

They were Church of Ireland scholarships to attend secondary school. I think they may still exist. My mother always gave to a charity called the Distressed Protestant Gentlefolk or something like that because she said she was sure she was about to become one at any moment.

We always found those kinds of societies fascinating.

I am fascinated by them myself. I think of the Sick and Indigent Roomkeepers' Society near the Olympia Theatre and I am so glad they have preserved it.

So you got a scholarship to secondary school. While you were there was it considered unusual that you wanted to go to university?

Not so much that it was unusual but only a small number went to university because money was very tight in the late 1950s.

So there you were finally in Trinity.

I didn't get a scholarship into Trinity, I got one after I had been there a year.

What was it like for you, a young Protestant girl called Mary, going into Trinity? What year was that?
It was 1958 and it was fine. However there were very few women in my year and not many Dubliners unless they were Protestant, because Archbishop McQuaid had banned Catholics from attending Trinity.

Were you happy in Trinity?
In the beginning I was quite frightened but I was lucky: I met a girl called Rosemary Harris from Donegal and we became great friends. We were put into digs together and we got on very well from the beginning. Sadly she died when she was forty-seven. She spent the last couple of months of her life in our house in Dublin.

When you went into Trinity was it for the specific purpose of studying medicine?
Yes, and I got on well. I enjoyed it very much.

And you graduated when?
In 1965. Then I went to work in what the locals used to call Saint Patrick Dun's Hospital. Sir Patrick Dun was the body surgeon of William of Orange and he decided that we poor Irish needed a hospital. He was a Scot, and he set up the hospital and the Chair of Medicine in Trinity College. I worked there for quite a long time. Also I worked in the Rotunda and later in the Adelaide.

Why did you choose Sir Patrick Dun's?
Because my grandmother, Frances Fraser Henry, and Constance Markievicz had died there. Not a very good reason to choose a

hospital. My grandmother became ill in Sligo and was transferred to Sir Patrick Dun's because her cousin Robert Rowlette was Professor of Medicine in Trinity at the time.

Both this and the Adelaide would have been perceived as Protestant Hospitals.

They would. But nearly all the small hospitals – Baggot Street, Mercers, Dr Steevens – were set up by small voluntary bodies of middle-class Protestants, although 90 per cent of the patients were Catholic. The other hospitals would have been run by the Catholic religious orders.

When did you marry?

In 1966. I met my husband in the Casualty department in Sir Patrick Dun's. He was very interested in cars – he still is – and he had cut his hand on the door of a car. It had been stitched in the hospital and he came back in to get the stitches out. I was very busy at the time and I think I gave out to him and said it was the likes of him who had the likes of me in a state of collapse. He asked me out but I told him I couldn't go out with him because he was a patient. I thought the Medical Council would strike me off if I went out with a patient. Eventually one day when I was again ushering him out of Casualty we met the medical registrar, Freddie Chen. Freddie had been at school with John and was a great friend of his. Freddie asked him what he was doing there and he said he was there trying to get this woman to go out with him, so Freddie introduced us. So then it was perfectly all right to go out with him. That's how we met.

And you married how soon after?

We married about a year later. We had three children within

a very short space of time, four-and-a-half years, and I was extremely ill on the third pregnancy. I had developed Addison's Disease but nobody realised what had happened to me and I spent most of that pregnancy in the Rotunda. While I would have liked to have more children I felt that the mother my children *had* might be better than an unknown stepmother.

It is interesting that you say you would have liked to have more children because once again the perception would be that Protestants had small families.

Well, some did and some didn't. I wonder sometimes how Protestants managed to have small families in those days because contraception was unobtainable.

How did your political involvement begin?

One of Mary Robinson's brothers, Ollie Bourke, was in my year in college, and I was very friendly with her other brothers as well. When Mary decided to run for the Seanad, in 1969, she asked me if I would I give her a hand and I said of course I would.

I remember to this day meeting her outside Trinity. She said she was going to look for the legalisation of contraception. Now I did not want to appear to be a lily-livered coward and I leaned against the wall and said, 'Of course, Mary, if that is what you want to do.' She ran a good campaign and got elected and I did a lot to try and get the medical vote out for her because the medical vote was very cohesive in those days.

She set off trying to get contraception legalised. I remember when she first had her Bill – supported by Trevor West and John Horgan, who were university senators – on the order paper, the then Leader of the Seanad would not hold the order paper in his hand. I had read some of the debates from those days and they were beyond belief.

I was working in the Rotunda at the same time and I had to deal with women who had deep-vein thrombosis and complications like that. Some of them had varicose ulcers and others were women in their thirties and forties who should not have been pregnant at all. They were on their sixth, eighth or tenth pregnancy and many had rheumatic heart disease as well. The place to go to hear really bad heart murmurs was the maternity hospitals. It was quite shocking to listen to these women. Mitral stenosis, mitral incompetence, aortic stenosis, aortic incompetence: these women just died. In Ireland twenty or thirty women died annually in association with pregnancy. I found this very distressing. These women, who should not be pregnant at all, were forbidden to get any advice on contraception. The pill was available as a cycle regulator, but that was really unsuitable for these women. It was the high-dose pill with risks involved and these were already high-risk women.

I went to where the records of the maternal deaths were kept and a very nice man called St John Cowell said he would go through them with me but I couldn't look at the names. I didn't want to look at their names or who their doctors were; I just wanted to get their ages, what medical conditions they had, the number of children they had and what they had died of. I produced a paper eventually which showed that at least 50 per cent of the women who died of pulmonary embolism had six or more children, about a quarter had ten or more and most of them were over thirty-five. I published this paper in the *Irish Medical Journal* and no one even commented on it. I presented it in the College of Obstetricians and Gynaecologists in London and when I started talking about a woman of forty-seven who was on her seventeenth pregnancy and who was an epileptic into the bargain and who had died, I could see that the audience stopped believing me. But I was telling the truth. This was only thirty-five years ago. This was going on in Ireland.

This was a time when, for Catholics, it was considered a mortal sin to use contraception.

Exactly. The Catholic bishops used to talk about a 'contraceptive mentality', whatever that meant. Austin Clarke wrote an interesting poem about this, 'The Redemptorist'. In the poem the priest asks this woman why she is not having more children and she tells him that the doctor told her she shouldn't have any more – she has five. The priest says that she must not abstain from sex with her husband. That Saturday night she feels her husband's weight like a coffin lid on her.

I read that poem into the record of the Seanad shortly after I was first elected in 1993 because we were still having trouble about contraception – this was in the early 1990s! There is such concern now, thank God, if a woman dies in childbirth. Some deaths are unavoidable but we really have to focus on this all the time. Into the 1990s it was very difficult for women to get effective contraception in many parts of Ireland even if they had serious medical problems. Do you remember Mr Haughey's bill, by which condoms could be prescribed by a doctor to married couples for bona fide family-planning reasons? Let us not pretend that this was in the dark ages. This was quite recently.

Were you ever afraid when you approached these issues on a political basis?

I would have to say I was. And if it wasn't for the fact that I had seen these women, I would not have done it.

You probably couldn't have done it if you weren't a doctor.

That might be true – I don't know – but the fact that I had seen these women had a profound effect on me. This is why I am so involved in the United Nations Population Fund: I feel we are still not doing enough about infant and maternal mortality.

You know the saying, 'All political careers end in failure.' Do you agree with that?

I suppose you and I got out when the going was still good for us. But there are some things that I am really fed up about. Ever since I got into the Seanad I have been trying to persuade the Minister for Health to legislate for the fortification of flour with folic acid. Folic acid, taken before conception and in early pregnancy, is very important in preventing neural-tube defects – anencephaly, hydrocephaly and spina bifida. These are very serious congenital malformations and Ireland still has a very high incidence of these defects. When I left the Seanad in 2007 the legislation still hadn't been brought in, even though countries which have a much lower incidence of these defects have brought it in. And all I can think of is that at least one thousand children have been born with spina bifida in that time and that at least 70 per cent of these could have been prevented.

The first responses I used to get were that it would affect the confectionary trade and that our exports of confectionary to the UK and America might be harmed if our flour was fortified. The health of Irish children was to come behind the export of Irish cakes and biscuits! The United States has fortified flour for years and we still don't. What is the excuse now?

Did you enjoy your political life?

Yes, I enjoyed it very much. I really only gave it up because to be honest I found it physically exhausting. If you want to get anything done in politics, as you know yourself, you have to put in an enormous amount of work. You have to put down amendments to Bills and argue them, take part in debates on the issues you are interested in, put down adjournment debates, attend committee meetings and go to meetings outside the Oireachtas. I found that by mid-afternoon, in particular, I was in a state of collapse. It wasn't that I felt mentally tired; I was physically exhausted. I wonder sometimes if the Addison's Disease wasn't relevant to my tiredness.

How were your relationships with your colleagues in the Seanad? I know you were very friendly but you would have been seen as a controversial kind of person.

When I got in there first they thought I was very controversial but I think after a while they were astonished that I didn't try to create mayhem or anything like that. I pushed everything I wanted to push. Probably the most important and difficult things were to do with the debates on abortion. My views on abortion are pretty conservative. I suppose if I had to deal with women who had had illegal abortions, which are the cause of 25 per cent of all the maternal deaths in the world, I might not be quite so conservative. But I had a real struggle arguing for the legislation on abortion to allow the life of the mother to be put before the life of the developing child. To me it was just unbelievable that there was any opposition to this. The life of the mother should never be secondary. The developing child has rights but the mother has huge social obligations as well. There may be other children and she is a living person, while you do not know if you are going to be able to deliver a foetus/embryo that is still only eight weeks. Eventually the electorate agreed with my point of view but it took quite a bit of time. I think that was probably the most difficult struggle. Infant mortality and maternal mortality are the things I feel most strongly about.

So in fact you had a modest degree of success, which is, I think, as much as any politician can hope for.
I think it is as well. I think I did very well on the Veterinary Bill, the Copyright Bill, the Mental Health Act. I felt that my advice should have been taken more frequently on the Criminal Law Insanity Act. I was very pleased with quite a lot of them. I enjoyed debates on legislation very much. I am so delighted that the Trinity electorate and the Dublin Institute of Technology electorate gave me a chance to be in the Seanad because it was well worthwhile.

It was an interesting time because there were very real issues that needed to be addressed.
There were. Now people are addressing them far more honestly. As you can imagine I am disappointed with a lot of things in the health service at the moment: the delays in cervical screening when seventy women a year die from cervical cancer in this country. In comparison, in Northern Ireland, there is screening and a much lower death rate. Also the delays in rolling out breast cancer screening. I am very pessimistic about the way private medicine is coming to be relied on because this country is too small to set up Mayo Clinics at every corner. I have seen private medicine in America, and this seems to be what is being sought. It is not all Mayo Clinic standard I can tell you.

Many women in political life came from jobs where, unlike you, they would not have had a chance to earn a significantly high salary. What would your observation on that be?

My husband always asks me why I keep on giving up well-paid jobs to take on jobs with little or no pay. Senators are much better paid now but they would want to be – otherwise you won't get people to go into politics, which is much more full-time than people seem to realise. I think I did make quite a contribution in medicine. When Mary Robinson retired from the Seanad there were very few women there and I decided to run. We desperately need people in politics who are going to take a stand on what might be considered controversial issues.

There seems to be a reluctance on the part of the highly-educated young women to choose politics as a career.

I think you are right. It is very worrying. The hours in Leinster House are not the most difficult thing, but one has to keep up with an awful lot of activities outside Leinster House.

There is also the issue of personal privacy.

That can be dreadful. I never had much of a problem, thank goodness, but I look sometimes at the intrusion by the media into politicians' private lives or, worse still, the private lives of their families, and I wonder of what interest that is to the general public. If people are being really two-faced and saying one thing in public and leading another sort of life maybe it is of importance. But in general, people's private lives should not be of interest to the public at all.

So, for example, a bright young woman, coming out of college with a medical degree, might feel that she would prefer not to have the strain of running for election and, as well as doing her job, have a particular kind of public interest in her personally.

I think for a start that if she keeps going with her medical career she is far more likely to have a well-paid satisfactory life. Remember, Mary, one goes up for election every five years at the minimum. I was Mary Robinson's election agent when there were three elections in eighteen months. I will never forget it. And elections cost a lot of money into the bargain. So it would be very hard to say to any young woman, 'Come on, get into a political career.' I was fifty when I was elected and my children were reared.

Are your children interested in politics?

They are interested in politics but not in running for political office. We have marched all over the world against the Iraq war: one in Melbourne, one in London and three of us here in Dublin. I didn't even have to ask if they were going to march. In London, I knew Ralph and his wife would be there marching, Meriel was in Melbourne at the time and I knew she would be marching and there were Seán Óg, Mac and myself marching in Dublin.

And did they say why they wouldn't be interested in running for political office?

I would be a bit afraid to ask them. Mind you, they used to tease me when I went off to meetings abroad. They would say, 'There you are, off being a world person again.' I don't think they ever felt particularly deprived. My husband is interested in politics too. If you are a medical consultant, employed by the state, you can't get leave the way a teacher can. Moshee Bhamjee and I tried to see if we could get leave but we couldn't. He decided that he would have to go back to medicine and I decided to cut my losses and give up medicine and try to keep going with the Seanad. But if I hadn't got elected again it would have been very unpleasant, because I had had to resign my job. So when you look at all the elected teachers, they are in a lucky position.

Máire Hoctor

Tell me about yourself.

I am the eldest of four girls. I'm a native of Nenagh, County Tipperary, where I continue to live. I represent the constituency of North Tipperary. I was born into a small family grocer's shop and I believe it was my apprenticeship for public life. The customer always had to be looked after first. After my Leaving Certificate I went to the Pontifical University at St Patrick's College, Maynooth, and completed a degree in Theology and Arts. Then I taught religious education, some social studies and Irish in Our Lady of Mercy Secondary School, Waterford City, for six years, starting in 1985. In 1991 I returned to Nenagh and taught in the CBS Secondary School there. It was while I was there the I first became interested in politics at a public level.

Do you come from a political family?

No, although strangely there was once an MP for North Tipperary called Hoctor who lived in the area of Newport. But I haven't traced him. There is no doubt he was a blood relation because there are so few Hoctors in the country. One of the first things said to me on my first day in the Dáil in 2002 was when Minister Mary Coughlan told me I had broken the mould within the Fianna Fáil Party. Seven women had been returned for Fianna Fáil but I was the only new woman elected to the

Dáil and I was the only woman among the Fianna Fáil TDs who had not had a husband, father, brother or grandfather involved in politics before her.

You were the eldest in your family. Was it automatic that you were called Mary or Máire?
My mother's name is Christina; my father's name was Michael. My mother had a love of the Irish language and I think that was how I was named Máire. My name is Máire Frances; my father was Michael Francis. People sometimes call me Marie ('Maree'). They read it wrong and they put the 'i' in the wrong place.

Does having a traditional name like Máire make a difference in the way people deal with you?
I'm not sure. Often I am called Marie, and people mistake the spelling of the Irish name Máire. You would imagine that most people would know how to spell and pronounce the name correctly but I find that people spell Hoctor more easily. But I like my name It is probably what I would have chosen myself because I have a great love for the Irish language.

Does any of yours sisters have an Irish name?
No. There's Margaret, Michelle and Ena (Christina).

Do you think position in the family is an important factor?
I think our positions in our families is significant. I was the eldest in the family and I believe that this is an important factor in my having the confidence to go forward and present myself to the public. If you are the eldest you have much more interaction with your parents because you are the one longest with them and you hear the talk of older people. My dad died when I was

twenty-three but I knew him the longest. Also if you are the eldest you may be asked to look after the younger children so you have responsibility on your shoulders at an early age. Often you become the pleaser in the family and the others get away with murder! In any case, I believe position in the family is a significant factor in people taking on leadership roles. Being the eldest you become the leader in the absence of parents. The younger ones look to you for that leadership and you take on that role in an unconscious way.

Are you married?
No I'm not married.

What age were you when you were elected?
I was born in 1963 so I'm forty-four. I was elected to the Dáil in 2002, so I was thirty-nine. I was elected to the Nenagh town council in 1994, then in 1999 I stood for the county council as well and was elected to both. I was always interested in politics but I never thought I would enter public life. I believed I had fulfilled my ambitions by becoming a teacher. I wanted to teach from a very young age. Politics found me rather than my finding politics.

Were you approached by your party to stand?
Yes, I was approached by the Fianna Fáil party to become actively involved by joining Nenagh's MacDonagh cumann. They approached me again to stand in the local elections in 1994. I agreed, reluctantly; I remember it quite clearly.

Had you been involved in local issues at that stage?
No, but I saw the opportunity to give something back, having

received a third-level education. I was not the first woman to be elected to the town council and I'm not sure if I was the first woman mayor but I was the only woman on that particular sitting of the council.

I became involved in the Toastmasters' Club at home in Nenagh, which gave me the confidence to speak in public. This was a great stepping-stone for me and helped me along the way. Women are great at communicating their feelings to their peers, but speaking in public may be a daunting experience for them.

Was there support or resistance from local male politicians when you were running?

This is a difficult question to answer but yes, if I am to be honest, there was some resistance. I think politicians are often wary and resistant to change, particularly because of the territorial rights they claim once they become elected and established as public representatives. I can see why this arises because people work very hard to retain their seat on a council or anywhere else and if there appears to be a threat that is a difficulty that has to be overcome. But we as members of a Party, like all Parties, have to keep renewing our membership and bringing in younger people. It is about keeping that balance and also welcoming new ideas and new experiences around a council table.

Did you displace someone to get your seat?

At council level, no, we won additional seats. And at Dáil level certainly not: Michael O'Kennedy was retiring after thirty-five years so I suppose his seat was seen as a Nenagh seat within North Tipperary. And I was happy to take it.

I've heard it said that people are easier on you if you have a nice plain name. Do you agree with that?

That is a very interesting point. I know you mean my Christian name but I would like to concentrate on my surname for a moment. I think we would have to be honest and say that it is extremely helpful to have an unusual surname, like your own surname of Banotti.

Absolutely.

Because there are not too many Hoctors and not too many Banottis and this *does* make a difference, meeting people socially and certainly on the ballot paper. Even if you are at the end of the ballot paper it makes you clearly identifiable when people go to vote. The name Hoctor is advantageous because it is unusual and stands out.

I have great admiration for John Ryan, who was a Labour TD in North Tipperary for many years. Now there must be hundreds if not thousands of John Ryans living in Ireland and certainly a lot of them living in Tipperary but John Ryan made an indelible mark on the political landscape of North Tipperary.

People in my constituency are familiar with me because they remember me growing up. I believe one of the greatest assets is to stay among the people of your own community and represent them. It must be difficult for people who are trying to represent people in a community that they were not born into, because the Irish psyche is very much community-based. That keeps us rooted.

When people meet you on the street what do they call you?

I am called Máire without a doubt. 'Minister' really doesn't enter into it. People from a business background or officials in local government might address me as 'Minister' out of courtesy, but among my own people I am Máire and I am happy with that.

Except perhaps for Bertie, you don't usually hear male politicians referred to by their Christian names, do you?

Now that you mention it, no. It's advantageous to Bertie that he has an unusual Christian name. Sometimes the men have nicknames or their names are shortened; sometimes they are referred to by their surname; among their own colleagues they wouldn't be referred to as 'Minister' very often.

How was life in Nenagh when you were growing up?

The streetscape of Nenagh was very different when we were growing up in the late 1960s and early 1970s; there were lots of family groceries. If you were to visit now you would see larger supermarkets and multiples. The little family shop is almost gone. Our family grocery shop was a hub of activity, run solely by my mother. My father was an oil salesman for Texaco so he would leave home early in the morning, with his lunchbox, and deliver oil, diesel and all kinds of fuel to farmers right across North Tipperary. He became well known because he was visiting various farms each day. My mother defied the custom of the time, when mothers remained faithfully at home. She managed to rear four of us without a yard or a garden, on the side of the street.

So you lived over the shop?

Yes, we lived over the shop. It was a community in itself where local families came and bought their milk and bread and butter. We had company and conversation each day. Several families would have had their groceries put on the 'slate' and they would be paid for at the end of the week or the end of the month: sometimes the wife would order the goods and the husband would come and pay. The companies operating in the Silvermines, like the Canadian companies Mogul and Macobar, were great employers at the time with over 600 people on their payrolls. To be able to say that your dad worked in the mines was really a proud statement back then. We had Canadian school pals who lived in our community and went to school and learned Irish with us.

Did you and your sisters work in the shop?

Yes, we all contributed. We often indulged in chocolate as well, much to my mother's annoyance. But we were always on our best behaviour in the shop because people had to be looked after. We formed good relationships with people, young and old, through the shop – relationships that have lasted to this day. We played hopscotch and other games with the children of these families; our playground was the street. A lot of them have grown up and moved away but it is a very vivid memory for me.

Would people have known your family when you started running for public office?

They certainly would. I visited many farmyards, particularly during county council elections, where people would tell me that my father used to fill the diesel tank for them. That was a useful connection for me, and people also knew me from the shop. My mother came from a large family herself, a family of sixteen that lived about twenty miles from Nenagh. My father came from the same parish of Lorrha in the very northern tip of County Tipperary. My mother started out as an assistant in local shops in Borrisokane and Portumna in Galway. She set up her own business when she married my dad.

After you were elected to the Dáil, did you find there was a difference between rural politics and city politics?

Rural politics and city politics are very different. That's one of the first things that I observed when I arrived in Dublin and attended the Dáil. The work hours are very different and I envy the TDs and senators who can return home at night during the week when they are attending the Dáil or Seanad.

Rural politics are very different. Often the legislation we pass through the Dáil is irrelevant to a lot of people in rural areas. They want us to legislate but they also want to see, literally be able to see us, back at home in the constituency. They want to meet us. They may not have any particular issue in mind but they want to see us at events, like the opening of the local school or the funeral of the schoolmaster. They want us to remain involved in community life. Issues like nitrate directives and sheep headage payments are serious business for us rural politicians. I didn't grow up on a farm, although I spent my summer holidays on my mother's and father's home places, but I became well versed very quickly in agricultural matters because it was expected of me as a TD. You are expected to know a lot of things quickly when you are elected to the Dáil.

Could you outline the main focus of your current job as minister for state?

I have been given sole responsibility for older people, which bases me in Hawkins House here in the Department of Health. This encompasses areas such as nursing homes, home care packages, home help and everything to do with older people's health. I also work in the Department of Environment and Local Government in the area of housing. Batt O'Keeffe is the Minister of State for housing but I am responsible for housing for older people.

Sheltered housing and voluntary housing are my area. I am also involved in the Department of Social and Family Affairs with Minister Martin Cullen, particularly in relation to carers who look after older people. I have some minimal input into pensions but that is a huge area.

Are your own parents still alive?

My mum is still alive. My dad passed away over twenty-one years ago.

You have obviously had a career all your life. Do you think you could do what you do now if you had children?

I think it would be very difficult for me to do it. I say this with great hesitancy because I know that you feel very strongly about the involvement of women in political decision-making. Of course I believe it is possible, but to do this kind of job well and be a good mother and a good wife would require extreme discipline and patience and a lot of sacrifice, both on the part of the woman herself and her husband or partner and children.

I have deep admiration for the women involved in politics because some of them have young children. It is an important issue because, while we have 13 per cent representation of women in public life at local level and also at Dáil level, there is a deficit of women in our policy formulation. When women engage in politics at this level they make a huge difference. Their commitment is unquestioned. I say this about all the women with whom I have had interaction with in politics. But I come back to saying that it is difficult for them. A lot of work needs to be done in the area.

They have now put crèche facilities in place at Leinster House and that may be useful. But the hours we work are very long and possibly people are unaware of the huge demands made on politicians. I would certainly not like to see the Dáil sitting five days a week. Three days a week is quite enough and we are there until all hours. It is a crazy existence in many ways.

Do you have time for anything else except politics?

Yes, I have a very good network of friends and I love to meet up with them. We might go for a meal, or just spend time together. I am quite an introverted person: I love my own company and I often just enjoy the silence of having no phone ringing. This is how I recharge the batteries to get ready for the next day.

Do you have hobbies?

I enjoy swimming. I enjoy music. I play a little bit of guitar – not as much as I would like. I like a sing-song and the socialising that goes on. I don't drink alcohol. I have never drunk alcohol and now I find it is a liberation for me that I don't because I always remember what I said the day before. Not that I want to cast aspersions on people who enjoy their drink: I have no problem with that either.

Are all your friends teachers?

Some of them are teachers, former colleagues of mine. Others would be longstanding friends who went to school with me and with whom I have remained in contact.

Would you agree with the adage that says if you want a good friends in politics get yourself a dog?

I didn't hear that one before. It must be a European one, Mary!

Do you have a special friend?

Well I don't have a dog. I have many friends. In politics yes, you have to be careful with those you trust but I have a few very close friends who help me with all kinds of decisions. I am very fortunate to have them and I enjoy my relationship with them. You cannot work in isolation, you have to work with people at different levels of trust and interaction. If you didn't have people like that in your life, it would be extremely difficult.

President Mary McAleese

(*I was unable to speak personally to the President. Her press secretary sent me her official biography,* The Road from Ardoyne *by Ray MacManus, from which I took the following biographical information.*)

Mary McAleese was born Mary Leneghan on 27 June 1951 in the Royal Victoria Hospital, Belfast, The Royal as it is commonly called. It was the feast day of Our Lady of Perpetual Succour so she was called Mary. She also had a grand-aunt called Mary Cassidy.

Family lore recounts that from the day Mary was born she was noisy. She made so much noise that the poor overstretched nurses consigned her to the bathroom. Her mother said, 'The nurses told me that Mary and a local golfer's son were the two noisiest children ever to be born in the hospital. They said that it was our bad luck that they both arrived on the same day.'

Mary's family came from Northern Ireland and from County Roscommon. She had a traditional Catholic upbringing and, probably because of the situation in Northern Ireland, the Catholic religion was a hugely important part of her life and that of her family – more so than any of the other Catholic Marys interviewed,

She was the eldest of nine children and throughout her childhood, living in the Ardoyne area of Belfast, she had very direct and personal experience of the tragedies of Northern Ireland during that time. She was educated locally and in the St Dominic's High School in the Falls Road. In 1969 she watched Catholic homes burn in the Ardoyne and her family experienced serious violence and many attacks on their own home. In 1972 the Leneghan family was forced to leave the family home, after an attack, and move into a safer part of Belfast.

From her teenage years Mary was very politically aware. Politics – or lack of political power – impinged on the lives of most young Nationalists in those days. They knew they were unlikely to have a vote in local elections if they still lived in the family home when they reached voting age. The government allowed only two votes per household but extra votes were granted to owners of businesses that had a rateable value of £10 per annum or more. Catholics traditionally had the larger families and consequently many more Catholics than Protestants were disenfranchised. At the same time Protestants owned 90 per cent of Northern Ireland businesses, some of which allowed their owners to have up to forty votes.

As a teenager Mary attended regular meetings of the Society of Saint Vincent de Paul and the Patrician Society. These meetings gave young people an opportunity to discuss a wide range of social issues, under the supervision of a spiritual director. In many ways they resembled an unstructured debating society.

Throughout Mary's life she was to break many moulds and in 1969 she was one of eleven women, from a group of fifty students, who entered Queen's University School of Law. There were twenty Catholics in her year, by far the biggest percentage on the Law course up to that time.

Mary's friends were a healthy mix of Catholics, Protestants and Jews. All except the foreigners had come from denominational schools.

Mary McAleese has always been a constitutional nationalist. Her family background was nationalist and her grandfather an unapologetic supporter of de Valera and the Fianna Fáil party. Like her father before her, she believes passionately in the republic as a political institution, in the principles of republicanism and the teachings of Tone and Rousseau.

In 1976 she married Martin McAleese, who has been a huge supporter and organiser in her life. She has taken courageous stances within the Catholic Church, particularly on the rights of women. When a group of women, including Nuala Fennell, decided to open the first hostel in Ireland for abused wives, Mary raised the issue and helped to establish a similar hostel in Belfast. In 1975, she was appointed Reid Professor of Criminal Law, Criminology and Penology at Trinity College Dublin. While she was working in TCD her husband Martin gave up his accountancy practice and qualified as a dentist in the same university.

When Mary Robinson announced in 1997 that she would not be seeking re-election to the Presidency, Martin McAleese and a close friend immediately saw the possibility of Mary becoming a candidate and organised an extremely active campaign for the Fianna Fáil nomination. This was a controversial turnabout as a former Taoiseach, Albert Reynolds, was also seeking a nomination at the time. She defeated Reynolds after successful canvassing of the Fianna Fáil parliamentary party and this started the Presidential election campaign on a very dramatic note.

Mary McAleese was elected President in October 1997. In 2004 she was appointed, unopposed, for a second term as President.

She and her husband have three children who are now young adults.

Mary Lou McDonald

Where were you born and where did you come in the family. Why were you called Mary?

I was born in Dublin. I'm a city girl, one of four children. I have an elder brother and then there is a set of twins after me, so we are two boys and two girls, a perfectly balanced family. I was born in Holles Street Hospital on Mayday 1969. I was due to arrive in April but I was late, as my mother never ceases to remind me. The plan had been to call me Avril but I arrived on Mayday so Mary was bound to be in my name given the month.

My grandmother was also Mary: Mary Black (Mary Hayes), known as Molly, so the name was in the family. My full name is Mary Louise, which just got shortened to Mary Lou. When I was a child I would very rarely be called Mary Louise unless I got into trouble. When the voice was raised and I got my full title I knew that I had crossed some line.

I had what I suppose would be a typical, happy middle-class Dublin upbringing. I went to school in Churchtown, to Notre Dame, a nice convent school. My siblings and I spent long, great summer holidays in Aherlow in County Tipperary, as my mother is from Tipperary. I always had a sense that, although I am a Dubliner, I have a second home and I still regularly visit Tipperary. We have a lot of family there.

My parents separated when I was nine and that was a

big disruption in our family life but it was something we got through.

Who did you live with?

I lived with my Mum; all of us did. It is strange because in those days, 1979, it was kind of unusual. There was almost…I wouldn't say a stigma as such associated with it… but it wasn't really something you talked about. Of course now things are very different but I think sometimes people still get anxious about children when marriages and relationships break down. Certainly my experience was that children are incredibly resilient and they manage. The main thing is that a child be happy and I certainly had a happy childhood. I was lucky in that I had a very good education, I went to Trinity College and then the University of Limerick. People say that you get lucky in life and my luck has been my family – my parents and my siblings – and the fact that I had a great education and a great sense of myself.

Did your mother work outside the home?

She did various things when we were a bit older. Now she teaches. She worked in a medical centre for a while. When we were growing up it really wasn't accepted that mums worked outside the home. Your mum was there when you came home from school, which was a great thing in many ways but very limiting. I know that now, as a woman in my thirties.

What did your father do?

Various things. He mainly worked in construction Now he lives in County Galway.

The Lou part must have given an exotic quality to your name? It sounds very American.

Since I have been knee-high to a grasshopper I have been serenaded with 'Hello Mary Lou', the Ricky Nelson song – to the point that when I was a teenager it drove me round the twist. I really hated it. Funnily enough, the other day I was on Parnell Street and a woman stopped me to say hello and she said, 'How are you Mary MacaLou?' This was a new one on me although I've been called everything from Mary Jo to Mary Ann. But yes, it is an unusual name and you can imagine that as a child having Lou as part of my name gave rise to all sorts of skitting and teasing and silliness, mainly from boys. I hated that. Fortunately I am past that stage now.

Did your family have a political background?

Well yes, I suppose our family would be republican in the broadest sense of the word. My grandmother, Molly, for instance, lost one of her brothers. He was one of the seventy-seven who were shot by the Free State [in the Civil War of 1922-3]. She was very political in her thinking, very nationalist, very old-style republican.

My own mother is political, too, although her interests – certainly when we were children – were always international affairs and what was going on in the world. So I would always have had a consciousness of what was happening around me. We weren't in any particular niche, although I would describe my family as having a Fianna Fáil background. But no one else in my family had ever run for public office so, unlike many women in Irish politics I don't come from a political dynasty.

Did you join Fianna Fáil?

I did. I was in Fianna Fáil for a short while. It wasn't while I was at university, as is sometimes reported. When I was in college I had no interest whatsoever in political parties. My view then was that individual issues were what mattered and that you had a better chance of seeing a result by working on an issue. And, to be honest, I was doing other things which I found far more engaging and interesting.

Like what?

Being with my friends, going out. I was involved in some of the societies in college but I never threw myself in hook, line and sinker, I enjoyed my books, I enjoyed my friends and I enjoyed the freedom of being at university. I was in Fianna Fáil for a while and I still have a great number of friends who are in Fianna Fáil but it was clear that I was simply in the wrong party. When I arrived in Sinn Féin I found that I was in the right place for me politically because my political drive is about Irish unity, ending partition. It is also about social equality and I found the blend of these things in Sinn Féin.

Did your family think it was very radical to join Sinn Féin?

I think some of them did. My direct family no, because they know me very well and they would have known my views. They also trust me and know that I am not rash or irresponsible. I am sure it gave cause for comment in my wider family; it wasn't something that they necessarily anticipated. Then, whatever about joining Sinn Féin, to run for public office was, as you can imagine, a big story among my family circle. But in the main people were very supportive of me and I think there is a particular respect for women who run for public office, because let's face it there aren't so many of us – that you take the initiative and put yourself forward before your peers and the people and set out your position. There is an integrity in doing that, I believe.

At what stage in your political career did you marry?

I am now married for eleven years so I was married before I was hugely politically active, before I joined Sinn Féin.

Your husband: is he politically involved?

Yes, inasmuch as he helps me out and is extremely supportive of what I do.

You keep him out of the limelight?

Well, he is not a party member. Martin is a private citizen and a fantastic husband and father. He works for the gas company.

Where did you meet him?

I met him during the World Cup, Italia 1990. A friend of his was dating a friend of mine, a Basque. But for that quirk of fate I doubt that we would have ever met. Martin is a little bit older than me. You say I keep him out of the limelight but there is no reason why he would be in the limelight. He is not really a shy person but he is very self-sufficient and self-contained and I don't think he would like the limelight.

Did you have your first child after you ran for election?

No, I had Iseult in 2003. She turned a year three days before polling day, I think. All in one transforming year, 2003-4, I had become a mother and all that brings and I ran for the European elections and won a seat. It is only now looking back on it I see how hectic that year was, and just how significant it was for me personally and politically. Then I had my second child, Gerard, in 2006. I was an MEP at that stage and that was an interesting experience. I went to seek information on maternity leave. I just wanted to know the procedure, so I spoke to the Parliament in Brussels and I was passed from the Parliament to the Houses of the Oireachtas. I have to say that all the staff in human resources were as helpful as they could be but, having spent weeks toing and froing, I was finally told there was no procedure.

There are very few people with babies so I suppose that is the problem.

Exactly, so it put up in big lights the fact that really women are relatively absent from politics – certainly women of childbearing age. It is just not anticipated that a Member might have a child.

Would you have allowed someone to take over your seat for a year?

If I could have I would have, yes.

Would you really? Most people, in my opinion, are justifiably cautious about something like that.

If there had been a mechanism whereby someone could be a substitute for me in my position for a period then yes. I think it is sensible that you would at least have the option of things like that. I made this point to the Parliament and I have to say the Quaestors were reasonably sympathetic on this issue. In terms of voting, why can't we have some type of supervised system whereby you could vote in your home Parliament if necessary – for instance, during the stages of pregnancy where you can't travel or you are on maternity leave or if someone has an illness that prevents them travelling by air. We live in a technological age and it is surely not beyond our wits to think of something. If you had women in sufficient numbers in institutions such as the European Parliament and the Dáil these things would be addressed because they would have to be.

Would you not be afraid that men who are fighting you for nominations would use that against you?

Well I suppose they could try. I took my full maternity leave when I had my baby and colleagues said to me, 'My God, we don't do that, politicians don't do that.' It was men who said it to me and I replied, 'Well, this politician does.' You are entitled to your family life. The fact that you are a public representative does not strip you of that basic right and also if we are serious about having more women and younger women in politics, about balancing political and family life, there is no point in saying one thing and doing another.

If someone wants to come at me on that issue and try to undermine me, I will very happily take on that battle. I think it is an argument we need to have within political parties and across the whole political system, if we are really serious about making women visible and about making it possible for women at every stage of their lives to be active in politics. Also I think the people I represent understood that I was about to have another baby and all that brought. I don't think ordinary people are so meanspirited or narrowminded that they ignore that kind of thing. Politicians aren't all that special: we are people who represent people.

Some women say that they made a choice not to go into politics – as I did because I was a single parent – until their children were beyond a certain stage. For example my daughter was fifteen when I ran. I don't underestimate that she paid a price as well. The prices of being in the political system are the vulnerability of women being out in public, the risk of people making comments and your children being upset by them.

I can imagine that this is the case. My children are still very small. With regard to my eldest child, Iseult, I think the only effect on her so far is that she thinks it is entirely normal that I go out and chat with everyone and people stop and talk to me on the street, which is a nice thing in a sense. But yes, when you run for public office and put yourself out there your privacy is completely compromised. You become public property. People want to talk to you and also as a politician you want to be out and about, meeting people. There is a price to be paid. Then in terms of being elected to the European Parliament, as you know, there is a lot of travel and away time involved. This is something that needs to be very carefully managed. I know my husband carries an awful lot of the burden of it and I am certain that I couldn't do this job without him. I am very fortunate that I have his support and that of my broader family. If I didn't have this support, frankly I wouldn't be sitting here talking to you now; it's as simple as that.

You belong to a political Party with a lot of very high-profile controversial people. Is your life quite different from what it would be in one of the bigger, more traditional Parties?

I would imagine so. It has always been very clear to me, when I am interviewed about something, that I would be approached in a different way from other politicians. Sometimes accusations are thrown at me that I don't think I would face at all if I were running for another Party. I think that is just a statement of fact. I also think it is largely unfair but I do accept that I am in Sinn Féin. The Northern conflict, the very long war that happened, is a fact. People were deeply hurt on all sides as a result and there are legitimate questions to be put. I have never had an issue with that. It is something that you anticipate as a Sinn Féin representative. But I think then what can happen is that journalists or other politicians – for all sorts of reasons, for their own comfort largely – zero in on one or two issues and bang the drum on those rather than taking in the scenario as a whole. I never have a problem with anyone putting any question to me or criticising us, or probing us – that is entirely as it should be. But I do have a difficulty when things are loaded and one-sided and selective. Very often that is the frustration for me.

But your background would not be that different to mine?
No, true.

Do you have any close friends in politics?
I have lots of them. They would tend to be from within Sinn Féin. although I would also be on good terms with people from outside my own party. Bear in mind that I have been an elected representative now for only three-and-a-half years which in relative terms is very short. But I think that, over time, both in the Oireachtas and the European Parliament, people from across the parties – women in particular – build a respect and a bond and even friendship.

When I talk about friendship I don't mean the fact that you have a good relationship with them, I am talking about sitting down and sharing some of the terrors and the fears if you are having a rough time. It is only when you have been there that you realise how frightful that can be.
Yes, and I would have confidantes and friends I would trust 100 per cent.

Are they elected themselves?
They are not.

Would you agree that it is only when you have gone out to canvas on the mean streets that you know what it is really like?
Yes, there is no question about that.

When Monica Barnes was first elected in 1979–81, she said she would really be enjoying the work if it weren't for the jokes. What she was referring to was the sort of *lingua franca* among men in political life. Have you experienced that?
The boys' club? Well, it's there.

How do you feel about it?
I've been at meetings where I might be the only woman or one of very few women in the room and it is the classic thing that happens: the men talk to one another and sometimes they even cut the woman out of the conversation or speak over her. It has happened to me and I have seen it happen to women colleagues. You pinch yourself and say this is 2008 but there is a whole cultural phenomenon involved and it runs deep. We talk about this regularly: how do you overcome these barriers, how do you

address these things? The difficulty is that if you are the only woman or one of very few women in the room, you just don't have the opportunity to network and build that critical mass to challenge this kind of behaviour. Now, personally, I would not allow myself to be spoken over. You do have to assert yourself and one of the difficulties is that an assertive woman can be told she is aggressive. A while back a woman came up and greeted me and said it was nice to see me but that she wouldn't support me. I said, 'Really, why is that?' And she said, 'You're much too aggressive.'

They are saying the same thing about Hillary Clinton.
I could be described as various things, but I don't think 'aggressive' is a term I would associate with myself. Where is the line between being assertive and being aggressive? I think the line is drawn very differently for woman and for men. The truth is that if you want to achieve things in politics, if you want to be successful as a woman, you need to be conscious of these things, because that is how this world currently works. There is a huge need for women politicians, whatever our stripe, to start collectively to try and think our way through this and around it. I know various initiatives have been taken but there is still a need for some way that we can address some of these things. It is not going to be easy or something that you do overnight. Far from it.

You would have been perceived publicly as being groomed as the acceptable face of Sinn Féin. How did you feel about that? You must have been aware of that.
I was of course. To tell you the truth, when I ran for the European elections in 2004 all of a sudden there was a huge media focus and it took me by surprise. I had no experience of it and it is not

a normal position to be put in. So I had the process of trying to figure out in my own head how you do these things. I saw this perception of me being 'groomed' and the new face and all that, and it puzzled me on one level, but then I understood that a story had to be constructed. I suppose it was a neat kind of story to tell. Other than that it did not really have any effect on me; the only thing that irked me, as a woman, was the suggestion, sometimes said up-front and sometimes just implied, that I was maybe cute but not that bright. They were saying that this woman was being run because she was being groomed as the new face of Sinn Féin and she was respectable. And never a thought that maybe this is a capable person, someone who has the confidence of those she works with to go out and do this job. That irritated me but I suppose it was par for the course.

How do you deal with what is perceived as failure?

Well it is very difficult. I ran in the election just gone by [general election 2007] and to my horror the expectation was that I was a favourite, that I was a shoo-in. Let me tell you I never want to be a favourite for anything in my life again because it heaps enormous pressure on you and it leads to all sorts of assumptions. It was my first time to run in this constituency and I always knew how tough it was going to be and it was incredibly frustrating to be reading inflated assessments. But what can you do? You have no control over that. When the fateful day arrives and the result is disappointing, it is gutting, it is very difficult personally. If you run for an election you have to play to win. There is no sense in being in the field unless you are absolutely serious about winning. But, at some level, psychologically, you need to prepare yourself to be gracious in defeat and to be able to cope with it.

So, how did I deal with it? I was disappointed and a bit numb because I was very tired. Then I sat back and realised that it wasn't the end of the world and that I would live to fight another day. I wasn't particularly tearful, strangely enough, which surprised even me. It took me a couple of months to get myself back into the groove. Your confidence takes a knock and there are plenty of people out there to drive the point home and to give you several more knocks. I think it is a test of whether or not you should be in this game in the first place, because, when you run for election there is only one of two outcomes – win or lose. A lot of it comes back to just being fortunate in my own domestic life. I have two very small children who couldn't care less and have no sense of what an election is. I have the comfort of my home life and that is my safety net and once I walk in the door it doesn't really matter.

Did you go away after the election?

We went away to Spain for a couple of weeks with the children, which was lovely. That was several weeks after the election. It takes you quite a long time to wind back down again because the hype and the build-up and the adrenalin rush are so intense and the campaign is so long, After the verdict is cast for good or for bad it takes you a couple of months, even physically, to normalise and to get a normal sleep pattern back and to stop obsessing over every detail and to settle yourself back in politically. When I won the election in 2004, all a sudden I was going to the European Parliament and my whole life had to be rearranged. On both occasions, having won and having lost, I found it an incredibly long process afterwards to try and get my head back together again.

Mary O'Rourke

Do you like your name?

When I was young I hated the name. I would have loved to be Assumpta or Concepta. I didn't know what Concepta was about but it sounded really holy. Goretti too, as there was a Maria Goretti. I think they would have been gorgeous. Carmel was another name that sounded gorgeous. But what really made me doubly hate my name was that I was a plain little girl. Whether I am still very plain I don't know. My mammy and daddy loved me but I was a plain girl and it seemed to me that the name Mary was for plain girls.

Where do you live?

I live in Athlone where I was born and bred. Lenihan was my own name and there were four of us in the family: Brian, Paddy, my sister Ann, then after four years I came along. So I was really the end of the family and I was given the names Mary Constance Hannah. Today if you met a girl or a woman called Constance or Hannah you would think what a brilliant name she had. My mother called me Constance after Constance Markievicz and Hannah after Hannah Sheehy Skeffington so she must have known I was going to be a politician. In class I think the nun took delight in saying, 'Please give your full name, Mary Lenihan.' I would say, 'Mary Constance Hannah Lenihan,' and the whole of third, fourth, fifth and sixth class would erupt in laughter. I never had long hair, because it grew out into a kind of a mop and I used to see Assumptas with pigtails, curls and ringlets and I thought they were brilliant people. So there I was, plain Mary followed by Constance and Hannah and I was a misery.

Presumably the nun knew you came from a Fianna Fáil family.

Yes, my father *was* Fianna Fáil in Athlone. He was chairman of the county council and chairman of the town council and he was an important guy in small-town Ireland. Along the way I dropped Constance, I don't know why, because when my university Seanad votes are sent to me now they come to Mary Hannah Lenihan O'Rourke. Also I am a Gemini, 31 May, and apparently Geminis are always having one over on people, pursuing several agendas and too big for their boots – double personalities. My sister Ann is lovely and quiet and when I went away to boarding school she was just finishing. They kept saying to me oh, if only you were like your sister Ann. I hated having this said to me.

But I think Mary is coming back now. When I was Minister for Education I would go into schools and say to fifth class. 'How many Marys in this class?' And there would be one. I remember going into a school and there was no Mary in the whole class. They were called whatever the name of the day was but maybe followed by Mary, like Charlotte Mary. But now I notice mothers with babies called Mary, so it is coming back into fashion.

Why do you think it went out of fashion?

I described how I didn't like the name when I was young. I think that's why it went out fashion. My mother would say it was lovely to be called after Our Blessed Lady and wasn't I a lucky girl to have such a lovely name as Mary. In fact Mary goes with any surname, when you think about it. Going through political life I was glad to be Mary. There weren't that many around but now there are lots: Mary Upton, Mary Hanafin, Mary McAleese, Mary Coughlan and Mary Harney. When I started in public life, it struck me that it was a good name, a name that people find it easy to use. Very few people call me Mrs O'Rourke and if they do I am kind of looking at them. I have found it very useful in the constituency because for some reason constituents are never shy of saying. 'Hello, Mary.' They don't feel it is rude to say the name Mary, which is very interesting. They feel familiar with you. Now I am very proud and pleased that I was called Mary.

Do you mind me asking how old are you?
I don't mind at all. I was born on 31 May 1937.

You obviously come from a political family.
All our lives it was politics and history and elections and people coming to the house.

Did you have civil war history?
Yes, a very interesting one. My mother's family, which was from County Sligo, was strongly republican. My grandmother was left aged twenty-six with six children and one in her tummy when her husband was brought home dead to the door after a pub brawl. She had twelve acres of land and no social welfare and she reared that family. She was a very tough, resolute woman. She was lucky to have a first cousin who was the reverend mother in the Dominican convent in Sligo. She took the girls in and they all got to Leaving Certificate. My mother and her sister May

both got scholarships to UCG, and my mother met my father there. He came from Clare, from a pro-treaty family; my mother was the republican. He stood as an independent first and then he joined Fianna Fáil. It was always interesting in our family that my father was on the opposite side, while my mother was the republican.

What age were you when your father was elected to the Dáil?

He wasn't elected until 1965. I was twenty-seven and five years married at the time. He was always too busy doing things. My father attended UCG, where he got a BA and LLB. He then lectured for a short while in QUB and taught in Dundalk Grammar School. My mother taught in the Loreto in Bray, where my sister I later went as boarders, but they kept up with one another and got married.

Then my father entered the civil service and became a tax inspector in Dublin Castle. They lived in Sutton, where my mother had three babies. He came home one day and said, 'Pack your bags, Annie – ' he always called her Annie '– we're going to live in Athlone.' And she said, 'What?' I was in her tummy at this stage. He said that Seán Lemass, who was then Minister for Industry and Commerce, had met my father while he was doing his civil service duties, had been greatly struck by his sparkiness and had asked him if he would take leave of absence from the civil service and go to Athlone to start up a factory called General Textiles (Gentex). It was the time of protectionism and subsidies to Irish industries. A lot of industries were state-owned.

Do you see yourself as a woman politician or just a politician?

In 1977 I sent Nuala Fennell £5 when she ran for the Dáil and she wrote me back a letter. I always liked her. She gave an interview in *Hot Press* about women's rights and women's delights. Then she came down to a public lecture and she was great to have around talking about contraception. She spoke at a meeting in the Royal Hotel in Athlone and we were all there. The following Sunday the guardian of the friary gave a big lecture about women in general knowing their place in life. We were there to nurture, to be quiet. He didn't mention any woman's name but it was pointed. Nuala went on to be Minister for Women's Affairs.

I don't like the idea of putting women up because they are women. I think it is a huge insult to women. When I was elected in November 1982, Charlie [Haughey] became the leader of the opposition. He rang me on a Sunday and said he was putting together the front bench and said he would like me to be Minister for Women's Affairs. I was getting the Sunday dinner ready and reading the papers and I said, 'No, I don't want that, thank you.' And he asked why, and I said because I didn't want to be put into a cupboard with Women's Affairs written on me. And he said what about Education and I said that would suit me fine. I always think that I was very brave to tackle him on the telephone. I don't know what got into me; it was like an out-of-body experience. I remember meeting Máire Geoghegan-Quinn a week or two later. She is very strong but she said to me it was a wonder I got education when I was not good at Irish.

The death of your husband was a terrible loss for you, I know.

I miss him physically. I try to explain this to people and they say they understand. I miss him in the bed, I miss him to cuddle up to. I miss him when I get up in the morning: we would have breakfast together and we would have chats. I think we would have had a lovely life together later on.

What happened to him?

He had a heart complaint like many men and he went to the Mater for treatment. He had a bypass and he made great strides after it and seemed to be OK. He had four or five very good years and then, around Christmas, he started to have vague pains and was going up to the Mater again.

I was giving prizes at a point-to-point on a beautiful bright January day. At five o'clock when I came home he said to me he had taken clothes off the line and posted letters I had on the hall table and he said we would have organic chicken. He asked me if I would do stuffing because he loved my stuffing. I said I'd put the chicken in and we'd look at the news and go up and have a drink in the local and all would be ready when we got back. I heard a noise in the kitchen and I came back out and he was in the chair. I said, 'Are you all right?' and he said of course he was all right and I thought maybe I had imagined it. But next thing he just fell on the ground.

We were married for forty years. We had had an anniversary celebration at the Hodson Bay Hotel with close friends and family. We were lucky to have had so many years together and to have had two lovely children who are now with lovely women and have lovely children themselves. And I was in the Seanad and life has to go on. When I went for the Dáil nomination again I was thinking of Enda and how he would have wanted me to get in again. I felt I let him down. He was dead, you see, when I lost the seat.

I do have to tell you that when I talk to people about doing this book, they all say they love you.

How kind of you to say so.

Why do they love you?

I think it is a) that I have survived as long as I have and b) that I have reached an age where I can be as outrageous as I like in my comments. I have lost all decorum – that is the best way of putting it – and I say it out as it happens. I find it really raises an echo: people email and send letters and calls come. So I am going to continue to be outrageous, not in an eccentric way but in a commonsense way, pointing out what is wrong and what is stupid in what people are saying.

Don't you like to be a little bit eccentric?

Well I am not quite eccentric enough because the long years of political life, as you know yourself, breed caution deep into your bones and I am only escaping from it.

That, I think, is a characteristic of all the women politicians. I immediately recognise it because I have it myself.

In spades. You were always very open. I was always inclined to be open and to be frank but it has magnified. Women see the absurdity of a lot of the carry-on, for example those bureaucratic pyramids like the HSE. Just give me someone who will tell me what is happening. But no, you are passed from A to B to C to D, all invariably male. There is a wonderful woman who keeps me sane in what was the Midlands Health Board area: she is based in Mullingar and she is the best woman bureaucrat I ever met. But mostly they are males and all you hear is, 'I'm responsible for dotting Is,' and 'I'm responsible for crossing Ts,' and 'Don't you cross into my space, thank you.' It's all a load of tosh.

Can we talk a little bit about relationships within politics.

Well politics is an exclusive club. You know the members' bar [in the Dáil] is open to men and women. I don't go into it very often but if I do I go into the public bar to meet someone. But if you go into the other bar the guys are all lined up, as they are in any bar. You always feel they have their code, you know the Patrick Kavanagh line, 'the wink-and-elbow language of delight'. As a woman you are a fully-fledged member but you wonder what you are doing there.

Political relationships are very rarely founded on friendship, but on necessity or propinquity, like being on the same corridor with someone for years. I have one very particular close friend in politics, a member of the Seanad, but by and large my friends tend to be outside the political system. I have a group of friends in Dublin and a group in Athlone. I have a social network, maybe not huge but tried and trusted. We go to plays here in Dublin – that is our big thing. Then I go home to Athlone and I have women and men friends there and we plan our Saturday nights out together. So I am not a political anorak in that I don't do anything else. I do.

I have been very lucky with relationships within politics. My brother Brian was a Minister when I was first elected. He was eight years older than me so he was a long way from my experiences but I always had huge respect for him and great love. I was very sad when he went. But now my relationships with my nephews are wonderful: young Brian and young Conor as we persist in calling them. It is almost like having your sons in the Dáil in that I really like them physically and love them. I meet them very often, not in an arranged way but in the corridor, in the hall, in the Dáil itself, the bar or restaurant. We always stop and talk. I admire Brian for his sagacity and his coolness. I admire Conor for his vivacity, which gets him into trouble. But I recognise a lot of myself in him because he refuses to be beaten down by the political system. He is funny and bright and very intelligent but succeeds in masking it, the intelligence I mean.

Being part of a political dynasty, did you see inevitability about going into politics?

I wanted to go. There was no such thing as a sea washing over me. We may not have talked much of my dear mother. She was a marvellous woman, who got first place in Ireland in her Leaving Certificate in French and History and then went on to get first place in Ireland in her BA. She was so learned, academic and intelligent and a huge republican. She was a really great woman and I think I never paid enough tribute to her. No, there was no inevitability. I wanted with my two hands wide open to be a politician.

And were you hurt, particularly by some of your public reverses in politics?

Of course I was. I cried my eyes out. I am a crier in private and I take things very much to heart. I reflect and sulk and pound the ground. I suppose I have got a bit more mellow about it. I have been very put back by those reverses but luckily for me, I will not lie down. I just refuse to. When I went forward for the last general election, people were writing to me and emailing me: isn't it lovely that you have all your grandchildren. Why don't you stay at home and be a good grandmother (or granny). I can't stand the word granny. Luke, one of my eldest grandchildren, who is nearly five, says dismissively to everyone, 'No she is not my granny. She is Mary. Everyone calls her Mary.' And other people suggested I go on a cruise. So I said, 'No thank you. I don't want a cruise. I want to be involved.' But for all those who didn't want me to go on, as many more wanted me to go on, so

I went forward.

I took huge risks. Firstly I took a risk at the convention, a massive political risk. There was a councillor, a good bloke, who was contesting, fair enough. I went into the convention with gusto and I won the nomination and then I had to win the seat. I could be sitting at home counting my grandchildren but I felt from the very beginning that the people of the constituency were sorry for what had happened to me and that they would support me on this occasion. And they did.

No, there was never inevitability about my political life. My father was twelve years dead when I ran for the Dáil so it wasn't that I slipped into his seat when he passed away. I was asked to run but I had two very young sons – Fergal was four and Aengus was five months – and I did what no feminist would do. I said, 'No, at this point I want to be at home with my children.' And I didn't do it. I have never been sorry for that. I was there for their critical years and Enda was there for their secondary-school years, making sure study was done and football matches were gone to and all that. So I think I achieved a bit of balance in my home and public life.

Monica Barnes memorably said she loved being elected except for the jokes among the men. Do you remember that?

I do remember her comment. I can say I haven't felt discriminated against or excluded because I just walk away if the conversation gets like that. I am not part of it. But men do talk a different language, and women see the nuances of a word or a sentence where men don't: for them it is black and white. I think it all goes back to when you are a mother, getting up in the middle of the night to feed babies and getting children to school and juggling the budget as we all did when we were younger. We have money now but nothing to spend it on. Also arbitrating in fights, standing in for dad and the whole thing. So I think women are multi-faceted in our approach to things and this approach extends to negotiation. When I am presented with a 'No' about something I always say, 'There might be another way around it.' You keep worrying away at things until you get an avenue to open to you. I think this is very important.

You said there, 'We have money now but nothing to spend it on.' What do you mean by that?

My husband Enda had a very ordinary job. He was a traveller for Jacobs and I didn't teach for a number of years, so we were living on his salary and we didn't have a lot of money. Of course we had enough to feed the children and a nice house and all that. Now there's much more money around but your attitude to money changes as you get older.

And now?

I'm very content with my life. I've two fine sons, five adorable grandchildren and a job I love, with the approval of my people.

Mary Robinson

Mary Robinson, née Bourke, was born on 21 May 1944 and christened Marie Thérèse Winifrid. Her father, Aubrey Bourke, was a GP in Ballina, County Mayo. She was the third child and only girl in a family of five. 'A family's not right till there's a Mary in it,' Mary's mother is reputed to have said before her birth.

Her mother, Donegal-born Tessa O'Donnell, had also qualified as a doctor and practised before her marriage. She was a strong force in the marriage and the home: 'very warm, dominant', according to her daughter. Mary was influenced by her grandfather, H. C. Burke, who had been a solicitor in Ballina.: 'He was a great fighter in court…It mattered very much to me that he had a moral approach. I was looking for very high standards at that stage.'

She went to school in Paris for a year after finishing secondary school in Mount Anville, a well-known girls' school in Dublin. According to Mary, 'What Mount Anville did for me was to encourage idealism, high personal standards of integrity.'

The intellectual, questioning life Mary Robinson developed in Paris made her independent and also estranged her from her parents:

> I recognised early on that I had gone on a journey that they would never go on, that would distress them if I tried to bring them with me, and which, at the end of the day, just wasn't necessary. I had an extremely good relationship with my father and mother despite that. And I just decided that I would cease to try to have communication on that level because there was no purpose to it and it would hurt.

Mary Robinson took a liberal line on the separation of Church and state as a law student in TCD in the late 1960s. After completing her degree in law she was called to the Bar. She received a scholarship to study at Harvard Law School and on her return to Dublin was appointed Reid Professor of Criminal Law in Trinity College. She stood for the Seanad election for TCD in 1969 and was the first woman to represent TCD in the Seanad. She was elected first woman President of Ireland in 1990 and served in that office until 1997.

I met Mary Robinson during her frenetic programme on a visit to Dublin in December 2007. We discussed her current work in the area of human rights and in the area of gender-based violence. She had recently returned from Chad, as Chair of Realizing Rights: the Ethical Globalization Initiative. and is now passionately campaigning for protection of the people on the Chad border with Darfur. She spends a significant part of her time travelling internationally, usually alone or with one other person. Her campaigns will always draw Press attention because of her international record and, despite her personal reserve, she uses this attention to highlight the need for action on these issues.

Where did your name come from?

I think I got my name [Marie Thérèse Winifrid] because my mother had assumed I would be the only girl and she gave me as many names as she could. I have always been known as Mary and am still addressed as such whenever I am out and about in Ireland. I am the third in a family of five children. I was called after my mother who was Thérèse [Tessa] and my grandmother [maternal] was Winifrid. I am always called Mary both within the family and out and about.

When did you become politicised?

I suppose I became politicised through my study of the law as an undergraduate and my brothers were also in law and had great concern for equality, justice and human rights. I had an aunt who was a nun in India and she kept us informed of the appalling poverty she was encountering while working there. I also went to school in Mount Anville, where there was a strong emphasis on service and human rights.

When people are asked their opinion of you, it is almost universally said that you are brave, shy and determined. Are you still brave, shy and determined?

Yes, I am shy. You would probably also say I am reserved.

How did you handle the huge public profile you had?

I did find it quite a burden to be always first and I had to overcome this when I was campaigning for the Presidency because again and again people said, 'We want someone who will do us proud.' My family was always supportive, and Nick particularly.

How did your children feel about the publicity?
We tried to keep the young ones out of the public eye.

How did you face losses during your political campaigns?
The first election I lost was very tough because it was partially as a result of an inside battle in the Labour Party. But it did make me very determined. Ironically if I had been elected I would probably have stayed in Dáil Éireann and never run for the Presidency. It was my first encounter with insider back-stabbing and it was very difficult.

The second election was less traumatic; my third child was born about three weeks before that election was called. So a lot of the organisation of the campaign concerned trying to find 'safe houses' in order for me to feed my baby. During this election I was already a senator and after the election was over I returned to the Seanad.

You took on some very difficult issues. How did you feel about the awful things that were said during the contraceptive debates where you were excoriated for bringing up issues like this in a public life?
I had been trained in Harvard and I had learned a great deal. Also that if you were determined to go after something you inevitably had to pay a price.

Extra biographical material from Olivia O'Leary and Helen Burke, *Mary Robinson: The Authorised Biography* (London: Hodder & Stoughton, 1998) and Lorna Siggins, *The Woman Who Took Power in The Park: Mary Robinson* (Edinburgh: Mainstream, 1997).

Mary Upton

Tell me a bit about yourself.

I'm sixty-one. I'm not married and I never was. I'm the Labour Party TD for Dublin South Central.

When were you first elected to the Dáil?

It was in the by-election in 1999, after my brother Pat, who was a sitting TD, died suddenly. I was re-elected in 2002 and again – with much gratitude to the people of Dublin South Central – in 2007.

Where were you born?

In west Clare in a place called Derrylough. It's a tiny townland near Kilrush.

How many were there in your family?

Three: my late brother Pat who was older than me, then me and then a younger sister Anne. Pat was a Labour TD as well. He did a degree in Agriculture in UCG and then a PhD in UCD in animal nutrition. He went on to lecture in the Veterinary college but he was always interested in politics.

When he was a student he was working part-time in the creamery where my father was a creamery manager. The workers were very badly paid and had bad conditions and they went on strike, Pat was working there for the summer and, as he said himself, he put steel in their backbone. It was his first exposure to real politics and what it is like not to have a good trade union. Then he went into student politics and was later elected to the Seanad. Finally he was elected to the Dáil in 1992 and again in 1997 but unfortunately he died very suddenly in 1999.

My younger sister Anne was a teacher but is retired now, very sensibly. She is married and has four children. She lived in Tipperary but now she lives in Dublin.

I went to the primary school locally and for secondary school I boarded at Coláiste Mhuire in Ennis. All subjects were done through the medium of Irish, including Latin, you'll be happy to know. That's not, I think, unconnected to the name Mary because the name belongs to an era where people studied Latin in secondary school. I think it's a great loss but that's a little aside.

I went on to UCG to study science and did an MSc there. Then got a job lecturing in UCD in 1969 when I was twenty-three and I did a PhD at the same time. I lectured in Food Microbiology. I did all the usual things as a lecturer – the publications and research. I had lots of students and really enjoyed it. Then when Pat died there was discussion about who would be the Labour candidate for a by-election. After a lot of consideration, and I mean a lot, I opted to let my name go forward. I was selected and the rest is history from a political point of view in that I was re-elected from there on.

Did you ever think you would go into politics?

If you had asked me that when I was twenty-three and had just started lecturing I would have given you a very definite no.

Why?

I just didn't think that I was going to be a public figure, nor did I particularly want to be. But I was always interested in politics. My parents would have been interested in politics without being political animals as such. They were interested in current affairs, good community people, good local activists in the best meaning of that word, in that they would have a concern for their neighbours – but in a limited way.

Your father was the local creamery manager. Did your mother work outside the home?

No, not after she was married.

Why were you called Mary?

Well, I was the eldest daughter and I was born in the month of May. I suppose those were the two reasons. They don't make Marys any more, do they?

When is your birthday?

30 May. I was called Mary Elizabeth. My granny's name was Lily or Elizabeth. I am told she used to vote for the Labour Party in County Clare. She was a bit of a rebel by all accounts.

I was also christened Mary Elizabeth. My birthday is 29 May, Mary O'Rourke's is 31 May. There must be something about Geminis.

Maybe there is.

When did you leave County Clare?

I went to UCG as a student in 1963, so I was gone then really because my friends were in Galway, although I didn't realise it at the time. I always stayed at home during the summer holidays and worked just one summer holiday in Galway. Then I moved on to Dublin and that was it.

Where do you live now?

I live in Terenure now but I lived in Dundrum for twenty-five years. I sold my lovely house in Dundrum to move into the constituency of Dublin South Central which politically I think is important. I have a lovely house again now, although it needs a lot of work.

Do you live alone?

My sister and three of her boys live with me but that is all coincidental. I suppose it would be of interest why the lads live with me. Two of them are working so they would be your classic well-educated, well-informed, hard-working young men who cannot afford to buy houses.

How do you feel about sharing your house with your sister and her children?

I don't have any problem with it. It's kind of nice. I won't say they are very good housekeepers but they don't get in my way. It's great to have company. I do enjoy that. They are young and they keep me up to speed and put order on me when I start talking about what they would consider to be totally frumpy things. I think that is good. I suppose I like it too because I always worked with students of that age group. They all have the same influence on you: while you are not one of them you know about them and what makes them tick. The boys talk to me about sport and films and television. While I would have no interest in certain television programmes they say. 'But you have to know about this, it's important.'

What sort of life do you have?

You know as well as I do, Mary, that outside politics you don't really have a life a lot of the time. To some extent it's our own fault. You are constantly on alert, thinking, 'Why am I not somewhere? Why am I not out knocking on doors or canvassing or dropping leaflets or writing a paper on something?' I must admit that in the last five years I have become absolutely obsessed about being places, doing things, writing leaflets, dropping leaflets, worrying about where I should have been and what I should have been doing and I don't know whether indefinitely one can go on doing that kind of politics because I think it is bad. It's bad for me because I find that I don't have a life outside of it.

One of the things you find as well is that you tend to lose touch with your own friends. I used to play a little bit of bridge for example, so someone says, 'Play on Monday night, Mary?' I say I will and then on Monday at lunchtime it's, 'Sorry, I have a meeting tonight. Can't come.' You can well understand that if you don't keep your arrangements you can't expect your friends to sit around. It is not that I don't have friends; it is just that I'm not able to make the commitment.

I think that if you are married and have a family, or if you are young and want to have a family, political life makes a huge demand on your personal life. You don't see your children very often, unlike other parents with conventional jobs.

I recognise that I have a choice. I have an alternative career in UCD that I could go back to but I don't want to. I think you can't go back and you realise that as well.

You know the saying: 'If you want a friend in politics get yourself a dog.' Do you have a dog?

Very interesting question. I used to have a dog, I always had a dog but our poor old dog had to be put down recently and only this morning I had a long discussion about getting another. I am a great dog person, I have to say. I used to have a Labrador too at one stage. Mind you, dogs are a bind as well: you have to think about them if you want to go away for a weekend or if you are late home. There is someone in my house most of the time to look after a dog but you have to think about the poor old dog as well. But you are right: in politics, dogs are good.

Before you were elected, when you were a college lecturer, what sorts of things did you do?

I loved going out for nice meals with my friends. I loved having my friends in and cooking for them. I used to go on holidays, long weekends, preferably in Ireland. Normally I go for long weekends somewhere around the country. I'm still always going back to west Clare or to Wexford, Cork or Donegal.

Do you speak any other languages?

No. I am able to speak Irish but as with any language if you don't keep practising you lose the vocabulary very quickly. I am still well able to understand and read Irish. I have at times allowed my name to be put down for an interview in Irish and, so long as I have a fix on what is coming up, I am able to manage. I am not fluent any more, which is a pity, and I have often threatened to go back to the Gaeltacht for a week or a fortnight in the summer to practise a bit of Irish again. I would love to be able to speak some continental language. I have a smattering of French and I mean a smattering, because to go back to my schooldays, Latin was the subject.

How do you feel about elections?

I think coming up to the last general election I felt reasonably confident. Politicians should never admit that but I felt I had done as much work as I could do coming into the election. I was quite philosophical about it and I just kept going doing what I had always done without getting into a panic. I have to say I even surprised myself a lot of the time. Now my friends and family may have a different view of what I was really like but I felt relatively calm.

Had you worked in elections with Pat?

Yes. I was always a behind-the-scenes person – to go back to one of the questions you asked me earlier on: did I ever see myself in politics. I didn't see myself up-front but I was always there in the background. I did lots of canvassing. I used to do his clinics for him and was generally immersed in the whole political scene. I have to say I loved elections then. I think Irish people just love the PR system. We love the tally; we love the count. Apart from anything else about electronic voting, I think we would hate to see the traditional counting system going. I enjoy it so much. I even enjoy it for myself because there is great pleasure in watching boxes being opened and seeing a good vote coming out. Even when there isn't a good vote coming out it is very interesting to see where you didn't do well and usually you can make the connection as to why you didn't do well. It could be because someone else is doing really well there or because you didn't really work that area or deal with those people as well as you could have done.

I remember at one stage when I was in UCD and Pat was a TD, some of my colleagues were English and they were absolutely intrigued first of all that you could have access to a politician in the way that they had access to Pat through me. He was delighted to invite them into the Dáil and they were absolutely fascinated that you can walk in there, as long as you know a TD who will account for you. And they were fascinated by the availability of TDs. As we both know, politics can be very demanding and very trying, with people asking why weren't you at their meeting tonight. It's very flattering in one way and lovely to be recognised but in another way it is a huge demand.

What sort of thing do you like to read, other than political briefs?

If I had time to read, I know the next book I'd want to look at is by William Trevor; I forget the name of it. I just love the twist in the tail of his stories. That's the kind of reading I like. I used to read a lot of books but I really don't any more because you go home loaded down with papers and journals and reports and everything else. Holiday time is my best bet for a bit of reading. I do like something unpretentious, light, interesting and relaxing.

You said earlier on, 'They don't make Marys any more.' What do you mean by that?

Well, I was born in 1946 and I would say that perhaps up to the early 1960s, the names that were selected tended to be traditional family names or names of good Irish saints. Now the influence is predominantly television, and pop stars and the other icons have moved in. I love a bit of history and a bit of attachment to a name and insofar as I had any right to have views on the naming of any of my nieces and nephews the preference I expressed was always for the good old traditional. Family names appeal to me.

The reason they are not making Marys any more is that we don't have too many Marys that are seen as popular figures among the younger generation. We do have great Marys around. I'm thinking of Mary Robinson, for instance. But do you call someone after Mary Robinson? No, I think that the big influence over the past number of years has been television.

But why would you call a child Beyoncé?

Because I think the factors that influence the selection of names and clothes and of houses and of the front door and everything else now come very much from television. There you see Beyoncé appearing to have a fabulous lifestyle – whoever Beyoncé is. It's just what has happened: we have moved into being quite materialistic in our thinking and in our actions. I can't think of any other reason. In the same way you have the Natashas and Samanthas. My sister Ann, who was a teacher, was always able put an age on people by their names. You could see names drifting through the school years and as time moved on you could see the gradual influence of whoever it was who was important – film stars of the 1970s and then the 1980s. Names went with them to a great extent.

What sort of qualities would you attach to the name Mary?

I think Marys are very solid people. It's probably not the best word to use because I don't want to suggest big lumpy blocks or anything. I would see Marys as being substantial – that's a better word than 'solid'. They have their feet firmly on the ground and I think they might even have a little bit of fun in them – they wouldn't be too frumpy.

What age do you think Marys are now?

I don't think you will find anyone much under about forty-five. I would say predominantly we are forty-plus. None of my friends who have had a baby girl in the last fifteen to twenty years have called her Mary. I think the clock comes full circle on this one just like other names. I remember as a child that was how the name Katie was viewed: people had an Auntie Katie and Auntie Katie was always elderly and a bit staid and dull and probably wore a tweed skirt and a twinset. Katie is now such a posh, smart, chic name and there is also a fashion for names like Ellie and Mollie. If you remember Auntie Ellie and Auntie Mollie, for goodness sake, you wouldn't dream of calling children after them in our day. And we had Auntie Bridies and Auntie Josies too but those names haven't yet been rehabilitated in quite the same way.

What did you think when I mentioned the name of this book, *There's Something about Mary*?

It's very interesting because in my election campaign recently I was trying to find a slogan. I pottered around with a few different slogans that were given to me by a very good friend of mine who is in PR. One of the slogans she came up with – the one I went with eventually – was 'Some Politicians are Different'. I used that as my banner on a lot of my literature and on my big posters. But one of the other slogans she came up with was 'Some Things about Mary' – we were going to do five things about Mary. I just laughed when you rang and told me about this book. 'Something about Mary' – it's not original but it *is* interesting.

Did you see the film *There's Something about Mary*?

No.

Do you think there is a class element in Mary?

I think there is probably. I would see it as safe, secure, quite middle-class.

Even in rural areas?

I think so. Although probably not as much in rural areas, I would say everyone in rural Ireland had a Mary in the family or some version of Mary. You had Mary or Máire or Maureen. Maybe mother was called Mary so they called the little girl Máire or Maureen or some version of it. In rural Ireland I would see Mary as quintessentially Catholic, steady, unpretentious and substantial. I am just thinking of the Marys you will be interviewing at some stage for this book and visualising them. You know Frank McNally wrote a piece for *The Irish Times* some time before the election and he looked at all the Marys in the Dáil. All the Marys at the time were ministers or junior ministers bar myself and he said I had a wonderful excuse as I was in opposition. I don't really know what all their ages are but they are all forty-plus, I would guess. Looking across at the other benches you have Olwyn Enright and Lucinda Creighton – well they are of a different age-group.

Were you surprised when the Labour Party asked you to stand for election?

I think I was surprised that I agreed to stand, at myself more than anything else. I wasn't surprised they asked me because I think they were very anxious that there was an Upton voice because of Pat's work. People complain about dynasties but let's get over our concern about dynasties, if they can deliver. That is my attitude to it. It doesn't matter who you are. You can be part of what is called a political dynasty or you don't have to be, just get out there and do the job. They asked me because I was very involved behind the scenes. Pat had done a lot of work and, let's be realistic, the name is valuable from a branding point of view. So I reluctantly agreed to let my name go forward.

Once I had done that I said let's go for it, let's make the very best of this, let's go out to win. And that is what I did. So it was a by-election and it was a Labour seat and traditionally it is easier to win under those circumstances. I would never be so arrogant as to say that I took it for granted but I suppose it is like a lot of other things I have done. I said let's go out there, do what I can do and get on with it. After that, if I win I win. If I don't I go back to doing what I did before. It was my first bite at an election on a personal level so I went out to give it my best shot and I was elected.

In 2002 I was nervous because it was my first general election and it was a completely different arena. I certainly was apprehensive at that stage, but I was delighted to be elected.

I was surprised at myself for agreeing to do it and I can still remember where and when I finally made the commitment to my very good friend and election agent Niall Connolly. He was a good friend of Pat's as well. I had been resisting and resisting and saying I didn't think it was a great way to spend the rest of my days: going to public meetings and worrying about medical cards and housing and all the things that go with politics. I had a long chat with Niall and when we came out of the pub where we had had a cup of coffee he said, 'That's fine, Mary, we'll see you on Monday and get your name in.' And I said, 'Right.' So I won't say I was walked into it – that wouldn't be true – but I really did agonise about it.

How has your relationship with the men in your Party been?

I have found them very supportive. I think one of the things they did was to say, 'We have a candidate. It's Mary Upton. Let's go out there and give it our best shot for Mary.' They did that, I have to say. Now that would be a loyal band of supporters.

MARY WALLACE

Which constituency do you represent?

I now represent the constituency of Meath East which used to be the five-seater Meath constituency. It has now been divided into two three-seaters, Meath East and Meath West and I am on the Meath East side of it.

Where do you come in your family?

My parents had four children. My brother Thomas was the eldest, then myself, then my sister Ann and my younger brother John.

Why were you called Mary?

I think it was because I had relatives on all sides called Mary so it was a family tradition. My mother was Rosemary and both my grandmothers were Mary.

Do you think having the name Mary has had any bearing on your political life?

I don't know really. First of all, my father was Tom Wallace and he was a member of Meath County Council. He died a young man in 1981.

So you came from a political family?

Yes, I came from a political family. My father was a councillor until 1981. He died in his fifties when I was only twenty-two, and I was asked to go for the co-option at that stage. So if anything was in the name I think it was simply the fact that my surname was Wallace. When, later on, I got married to Declan Gannon I did not change my name for the simple reason that I think you can't sell the same person with a different name. So the name Mary Wallace has carried me through from the time I was twenty-two.

Were you married when you first went for the council?

No.

So that was your political *nom de plume*.

Yes, that was my name and I was many years in politics before I got married because I went into politics so young.

How old are you now?

I was born in 1959 so I must be forty-eight.

Mary Harney said that when she meets someone called Mary she automatically assumes they are over forty.

That is interesting, yes.

And the other quote I got which I thought was very good, was that Mary Upton said, 'They are not making Marys any more.' What do people call you when they meet you?

Mary.

They don't say Ms Wallace or Mrs Gannon.
No, I would always be called Mary.

That is a characteristic of all Marys. People do call them by their Christian names.
Yes, I think what is perhaps nice about the name Mary is that it is easily recognisable. Sometimes I have to admit that if people have names beginning with 'S' or 'L', I'll say, 'Is it Suzanne or is it Lorraine or is it Sarah?' In our business it is important to remember names and Mary is easy to remember.

Do you think people are comfortable with it?
I would think so, yes.

For the younger generation the name does not have the same familiarity as it might for people your age or older.
I still think it is great to have a simple straightforward name that people can remember.

Tell me about your political life before you were elected to the Dáil. You were elected to the council but you had another job as well.
Yes, I worked for ten years in Blanchardstown Hospital. While I was working in the hospital my father died and I was co-opted on to Meath County Council but I retained my day job because at that stage working on the county council was very much a voluntary commitment. My co-option was in 1982, then in 1985 I was selected to stand for the Dáil but the election did not take place until 1987. In the 1987 general election I missed getting a seat by 200 votes but I was elected to the Seanad that year. That

means I am now twenty years in the Oireachtas. I stood again in the 1989 election and was elected to the Dáil and we haven't lost that seat since.

I noticed you know exactly how many votes you lost by. You can always tell professional politicians because they all remember that.

Absolutely, yes. I think it is quite traumatic to go before the people and not be elected, as was the case with me in 1987. I was quite young at the time too. I would recommend that people go into politics young because I have been twenty years in politics and have loved every minute of it. I do think the younger people go into politics the better. People are not getting involved in politics young enough any more.

Is your husband involved?

He is involved in supporting me as a candidate. I was lucky with my husband. We were going out together in 1982 so when we got engaged and married he knew what he was letting himself in for. He runs the postering campaign during the elections and he is always very interested in hearing what is happening when I come home from meetings. Our son Tom is now twelve and because, like myself, he was born into a political household, he is very interested in politics and in what is happening nationally and internationally.

And he obviously works during the election campaign.

Both of them do.

It seems that children either love it or hate it.

One of the things Tom got into at an early age was doing the leaflet drops with us. We would do regular drops even outside election time. He loves doing that and lots of his cousins and friends come with us as well. He likes meeting people and I think that is great.

Was your mother happy that you went into politics?

Yes, my mother was interested in the women's movement at that time and was very much involved in the Irish Countrywomen's Association. She died young, in her sixties, and at the time she died she was the president of the County Meath ICA.

Was that before or after your father died?

He died in 1982 and my mother lived until 1999.

You have just one child. One of the areas that interests me is that the vast majority of the women in politics I have spoken to have no children. Did you find it very difficult coping with a small child while a TD or senator?

Our son makes such a difference to our lives because he is so involved in many local activities, including football. He attends the local school and keeps me in touch with everything, education-wise and sporting-wise and organisation-wise. When he was a small baby I did wonder, as I suppose most working mothers wonder, about whether he was affected by my career. But I was very fortunate that when he was two months old we recruited an excellent childminder called Deirdre Carroll. At that time she would come to live with us for four nights a week and go home to her own house for three nights a week. She is with us to this day. I think that backup is very important because if women don't have solid support at home from a childminding point of view, they can't be relaxed, no matter what their career.

One woman said to me, 'I don't ever hear the men in politics talking about their children; they are not worried about them in the way that women politicians are.' How would you feel about that?

I know the families of some of the men I know in politics and I talk to them about their children. I am interested in other people's families; I suppose it is a natural topic for me to ask whether their children are playing football and where they are going to school. But in any career, no matter what the situation is, I think a mother will always be concerned to make sure that everything is right with the children first. That is my own position. I have no hesitation in saying that it is important for me to know that my child is safe and well and happy in what he is doing. I work very long hours during the week like most of us do. I work from early morning until midnight five nights a week, but I try on a Saturday to be available for my child's football match or if he wants to go somewhere. We call that 'our time' together so you can spot us in a restaurant on a Saturday at lunchtime. That 'quality time' is really important for me and also for my son.

Could you tell me what your ministry is and what it involves?

At the moment I am Minister of State in the Department of Agriculture and Food, working with Mary Coughlan. I have special responsibility for forestry and for the whole new energy policy in terms of the farmers' production of energy crops. For me it is a pleasure working with a senior minister who is a woman. I think Mary Coughlan is a wonderful minister and I am delighted to be working in the same department. She is a great worker herself. That was a great experience for me in the last year and a half and I am delighted to have been reappointed to the Department of Agriculture and Food.

Before that I had five years' experience in the Department of Justice, Equality and Law Reform and while it was different from the Department of Agriculture and Food, I had an opportunity to work with lots of women's groups. I was able to work on the whole domestic violence issue and we achieved a good deal on the equality side of the department. I have had great opportunities and I think it is lovely to be able to help, whether it is on the Justice side, or now with rural development.

How are you on the whole question of the relationship with the Greens? I mean in terms of your ministry.

I think it is very positive. I am fortunate that Trevor Sargent has responsibility for Food in my department. I have responsibility for forestry so we can work together but separately. Over in the Department of Communications, Energy and Natural Resources it is Eamon Ryan's job to drive the energy agenda but he can only drive it so far if we in Agriculture are not producing what is required for the greener agenda. I think that the public are very receptive to environment issues at the moment, whether we are taking about our side of the Green agenda or the Department of the Environment. The public has really bought into doing more for the environment and I think it behoves the government to encourage people to do more and more.

How do you get on with the men in political life?

I hope that I have no enemies in political life. I think it is important for colleagues to work well together and I hope that I have a good working relationship with my colleagues whether they are male or female.

When were you made a minister?

From 1997 to 2002 I was in Justice, Equality and Law Reform and then on Valentine's Day, February 2006, I returned to the Department of Agriculture and Food as Minister of State.

There was a lot of what I felt was unnecessary negative comment about you getting this job as opposed to someone like Seán Haughey. I am sure you found that difficult.

It was media-driven. The media talked themselves into thinking they knew the Taoiseach's mind and what appointments were going to be made, and, when it didn't work out the way they predicted, they were most unhappy and then they drove the other agenda. At that time I got lots of support from my own colleagues, who felt the comments were very unfair. I don't mind saying that one particular magazine went too far and we had to have some legal correspondence in relation to it and compensation was paid. I think the media should be careful to treat politicians fairly. I got over this but I do feel for my colleagues who are treated unfairly by the media at times. We are all human beings and we work very hard.

Can I ask you about privacy?

Politicians are elected by the people and when we are out, no matter where we are, people will speak to us in relation to issues that are of concern to them. I don't have any difficulty with that. Whether I am shopping, at the races, down in the village, at the school, even at Mass, people can raise issues with me. I love talking to people.

Have you had your privacy invaded? Have people tried to doorstep you?

I think fair comment is always good comment and I don't have a problem with the media if they act fairly or if they look for a comment from me, whatever time it is, as long as it is reported fairly. The problem I have with the media is the lack of fair reporting, which I think is an important issue. If you are a public representative and the media want a comment from you I think it is important to be available to give your views on whatever the issues are, as long as they are reported correctly. People believe what they read in the papers and I think the media has a duty to report accurately.

When your father was a county councillor what else did he do?

He was a farmer.

Would you have been close to your father? Would you have helped him in his political life before he died?

I was close to him. I think that is probably why, when I was sixteen years of age, I joined Ógra Fianna Fáil. I used to go to meetings with my father, more for the company and because I was close to him. I enjoyed sitting at the back of the room. I also see this a little bit in my own son; I think if you are born into a house where politics is talked about you like talking about politics and hearing other people talking about it. None of us expected my father to die so suddenly, but when it happened people around him knew me from going to meetings with him. I had a natural interest in politics and I loved it.

Meanwhile your mother had her own kind of political life in the ICA.

Yes, she was very much involved in the ICA and she played pitch and putt and loved that. This sounds like we had an easy life but my parents worked so hard when we were small. In their latter years they had an opportunity of getting involved in these things. When we were children my father went to work at four in the morning, collecting milk from farmers around County Meath and bringing it to the dairy in Dublin and then coming home to do his own farm work. My mother and he later had a garage and a shop. But as the years went on they were able to get involved – my father in politics and my mother in the ICA and other organisations and this was great.

It is characteristic of everyone I have interviewed that they speak about how hard their mother and father worked, on the farm or in a small shop or whatever.

I think a family where the parents work hard is a good ethos to grow up in. We worked hard on the farm as children and we worked hard in the shop with my mother. My mother had the shop open from seven in the morning until ten at night. At ten or eleven years of age we were driving tractors and doing all the farmwork with my father, feeding calves and all that. There is nothing wrong with working hard even as you are growing up and I think it is an important point for today's generation to remember – that children should be participating in their parents' lives and working. We certainly benefited from the work ethic that was at home.

I did as well, because my father died young and there were six of us under the age of ten. What do you think is different about the young politicians coming up? I am not asking you to make a comment on people in your own party in particular, but in general.

I suppose it is hard to know what motivates any of us but I feel myself that I am in politics today because I work hard and because I worked hard on the ground and in the constituency as it changed. Some people can perhaps be elected without a grounding in local county councils or in local community organisations, simply because of the support that is there for their Party at the time. I prefer the background that I came from myself because I think I'm in a stronger situation and maybe my seat is more grounded in my constituency.

I was co-opted to the council so my father had the background there. Then I went on to work hard on Meath County Council and in my first council election got two quotas. We were all thrilled with this and these votes brought in additional candidates. Looking back on almost being elected in 1987 and then being elected in 1989, I know there are people voting for me today who have voted for me for twenty years because of something that I did in the community or something my father did. I think that deep-rootedness is great. Someone said to me this morning that I am very much attached to the local community and interested in community needs.

Mary White

You represent where, Mary?

My constituency is Carlow-Kilkenny, which is a big sprawling rural constituency bordering Waterford and Tipperary and Wicklow on three sides. I was the first woman TD for the party and the first rural Green TD and also I was the first woman ever elected from any party in my constituency so it was quite a big issue being elected in 2007.

You made several attempts, as I did myself, to get elected. How many times did you run?

Third time lucky. The first time, in 1997, there was a very small Green Party presence in Carlow-Kilkenny and I walked over 3000 miles. I walked all around the constituency for months on end and someone told me it was the equivalent of walking to Berlin and back. I had a pedometer on my leg so I know exactly how many miles I did. It was really to give myself a bit of media coverage and in that election I polled over 3000 first preferences. In the second election I got almost 5000 and the third time I got in.

Where you were born and who were your family?

I am a County Wicklow girl. I was born into a not very large but a warm loving family. Both my parents were teachers and they were very progressive and idiosyncratic. We lived in a big old house with a huge garden in Old Connaught Avenue near Bray. We had an idyllic childhood, which I think has stood to my two brothers and my sister and me. We really ran quite wild with our parents' support. They encouraged us to be argumentative from a very early age and to discuss everything, right, left and centre.

Where did you come in the family?
I'm the first girl. I have an elder brother.

How old are you?
I am in my prime. I am in my late fifties.

I ask that because Mary Harney said to me, 'If I meet someone called Mary I automatically know they are over the age of forty.'
Yes, she is probably right.

Do you have to be called Mary and be from the country to get yourself elected to the Dáil?
It is hilarious looking at all the Marys in the Dáil. When I was growing up, I remember asking my father why he called me Mary because at the time I did not like my name. There were so many Marys in my class; I think there were about seventeen or eighteen of us, all born in the late 1940s or the early 1950s. My father said to me, 'If you are going to have a daughter you have to name her Mary; it is a simple good name.' That is why he picked it for me. I grew to like it. At my boarding school there were tables of eight in the dining room and at my table there were eight Marys, absolutely amazing. We all came from rural Ireland and went to school in Waterford. My maiden name was Conan

and I am related to Arthur Conan Doyle. We had to have our initials on our napkin rings and everything like that. Nowadays you hardly meet a child called Mary. I wouldn't have dreamt of calling my own daughter Mary. She is Dorothy Ellen.

What do people call you when they meet you?

Well, I am always called Mary straight off. I think it is a comforting name, a very familiar name, I have never had it abbreviated. In fact I have had to extend it since I was elected because there is another Mary White in the Seanad. My second name is Alexandra so on all my documentation I'm Mary Alexandra just to distinguish me. I have always been known as Mary. All my friends call me Mary and I think in public life my constituents all call me Mary; it is a very homely name. Once when I was working in publishing I had to write an article in about half an hour to fill a space in a magazine. My boss said to me, 'Write about your name,' so I wrote about how I had come to like my name and that it really was the most adventurous, exotic name possible. I convinced myself and gave loads of examples from extraordinary travellers and entrepreneurs and writers I admired who all had the name Mary. I felt in tune with them. I grew to like it, although at school I must say I didn't like it.

Was your family Catholic or Protestant?

I was brought up a Catholic and went to a Catholic boarding school in Waterford which I absolutely loved. Having read all the Enid Blyton and Chalet School books, I was up for it. I had been to a local school previously and my parents took me out of that and taught me at home for a number of months, which was fantastic. My mother is a zoologist and I'm sure that the time spent at home with her walking the lanes gave me a great love of flora and fauna and eventually led me to join the Green Party.

Were you affected by the *Ne Temere* decree?

No, not a bit. Also at the time there was the ban on Catholics going to Trinity College and I remember saying to my father, 'Will I be excommunicated?' and he said, 'Not at all, my girl, in you go. We are not asking permission of anyone.' Within a few months the ban was gone. In our family it really did not cost us a thought and we were very open about our religious faith. Both my parents are – or were, as my father is dead now – very strong believers in whatever they were.

Mary Henry said that Catholics always assumed that Protestants had no devotion to Our Lady. She didn't think there was anything unusual about being called Mary.

I think she's right. My grandmother was Mary, although she was called Molly.

I have an aunt Molly as well.

I nearly called my daughter Molly because I think it is such a lovely name. My grandmother was a very severe, Victorian-style granny and she died when she was ninety-seven in wonderful health. She was head of the family and you couldn't meet a better person. She was always Molly Conan; she was my father's mother.

When you were growing up, what did you want to be?

I was a bit wild growing up. I went to a series of environmental lectures with David Cabot when I was about twelve and there was a suggestion box in the RDS and everyone was writing in about how do you recognise a crow from a raven and what colour is a fox's fur. I wrote in, 'I want to be you, how do I become you?' And my piece was read out and I was absolutely mortified. It was the first time anyone had picked out anything. I wanted to be an environmentalist like him. He read that out and I was nearly sinking underneath the chair.

Later on I was going to do botany and zoology in Trinity and then I decided I would do English and Spanish. Languages were a big thing in my family. My father spoke four or five fluently, all the Celtic languages. But I think I really wanted to be an environmentalist for all my teenage years until I switched to the more literary side of things.

Had you heard of the Green Party at that stage?

No, not at that stage, because the Green Party is only twenty-six years old. When I was in Trinity I was involved in quite a lot of campaigns, protesting every other day it seems to me, marching out of the library. That element has gone out of student life completely, which is a pity. Then I married in 1980 and we went to live down in west Cork in the middle of nowhere. My husband's name is Robert. He was brought up in Carlow.

We lived a very rural life indeed in west Cork. We fished, we shot, we baked, we collected fungi, we ate the wild vegetation that we knew was safe and we lived completely wild for about two years until our daughter was born and we bought a house. Then we moved to Carlow to a place under the Blackstairs Mountains. We live in an old rectory. It is a beautiful old spot. When we were threatened with an open-cast mine I got completely stuck into stopping it. It took over four years and we won.

I had no intention of running for politics. We had our own bookselling business and a child and had just bought a house and were busy growing our own vegetables and really didn't have much time for politics at all. But I was very much involved in community activities, like the mining campaign, water campaigns, I was involved in Earth Watch and An Taisce and various things like that.

When I was asked to stand for the Green Party I said No. I said I couldn't take it on. I was so shocked. They had to ask me two or three times. I remember I was very interested in Gothic cathedrals and I went to see a wonderful cathedral in England. A bypass was being built very close to it and it was absolutely hell on earth what it was doing to that magnificent bit of medieval architecture, I turned to Robert and said, 'Right, I'm doing it,' and a conversion was made. I stood in the general election and I didn't get in, but in 1999 in the local elections in a rural three-seater, I topped the poll, the first time a Green had ever run in the local elections.

Does your husband like politics?

He has always been very interested in politics and he has been instrumental in me getting elected.

How old is your daughter?

She's twenty-five. When I was first elected to the council, in 1999, she was seventeen. So it was great that she had a childhood free of it because of the way politics takes you over – you have to make space for the family. Having a husband who is 100 per cent committed to me and my campaign is really marvellous. I don't know how people who don't have supportive partners or spouses can manage. I imagine it would be very difficult.

It is interesting how few children, if any, most of the women I interviewed have. A lot of them don't have any. I have one. Most of them either have very small families or no children.
That is extraordinary.

When I ran for election first, which would have been in the early 1980s, we wanted to think we could have it all. But I notice now that very few women, particularly those in public life, think they can have it all. In other words, families and politics together are too much.
Yes, I think you would run yourself around like a little hamster on a treadmill. You can't do it all. You can only be good enough. I remember reading a book on child development by Bruno Bettelheim where he mentions the idea of a 'good enough parent' and I think that is it.

Do you have time for hobbies? Do you have any passions that you indulge on the side.
Yes I do, and I make sure I indulge in them. Robert and I are very keen walkers. In fact we just came back from Mull in Scotland because our daughter is over there. We had a lovely four days. I hadn't been away all during the summer because there was so much going on. We are keen organic vegetable growers, and we are passionate skiers, which isn't at all green, but we do love the thrill of skiing downhill. Faster, higher, blacker, deeper – that's the motto and that is the buzz. I come from a very athletic family and so does my husband and we keep very fit as a family, which is good, because we can do things together and this is very important. And we also enjoy the antidote to the hectic skiing – a peaceful walk in the mountains or along the river. Our holidays would always be walking in the autumn or skiing in the winter.

How do you make time for this? Do you insist on it?

Yes we do. If I get carried away with work, which is frequently, my husband yanks me back and says, 'We're going away; you're over-tired, you're doing too much; you're not thinking properly; you need a break.' That is very good. I know myself when I need one. You have to make the time. I find it very easy: once I put a break into the diary it doesn't move.

So we go away after Christmas for ten days and normally we would go away again at another time. For instance, we have nearly finished the Camino de Santiago. We have walked three quarters of it so we have about another week to do but we couldn't get away this time for various reasons, so we have that to finish. We have walked in Crete and we are going to do one of those GR [*Grande Randonnée*] routes across Corsica as well. But you can't do them all in one go because the constraints of politics.

Even though people say we are off all the summer, we're off only from the Dáil and we're working hard in our constituencies. So ten days in the autumn and seven days at Christmas, that's it. But then there are weekends and I try not to do anything on a Sunday, if possible, so that we can cook a nice meal together and go for a walk or go and visit family or something like that. I have seen and heard so many horror stories of what people in public life do by not looking after themselves physically and not looking after their family and I don't want to be one of those.

How do you get on with the men in your Party and in political life?

Great. Because the Green Party is a growing Party I know them all very well. They were so good to me when I missed out in 2002 and I became almost a virtual TD. I came up to Dublin once a week and we had our meetings and they were very encouraging of my campaign to get in and delighted when I did get in. They are all really motivated, highly involved in the Party at every level and live Green lives as best they can. Of course the whopping great change that came about recently – the huge tumultuous event of being in government with three of the TDs being ministers, two senior, one junior – that in itself has fragmented the parliamentary party. Obviously the ministers are off in their ministerial areas but we do meet regularly to discuss issues just as you would in a good relationship.

How did you feel about going into a coalition with Fianna Fáil?

Well, I hadn't thought about it in advance because we always thought we wanted a complete change of government. Then you know – it is a very trite thing to say – the electorate spoke and Fianna Fáil, the most popular Party in Ireland, was returned once again.

Were you surprised by that?

No. In the last week I could feel that Fianna Fáil were going to get in and we would maybe have liked a complete sweep but it didn't happen, and we were faced with the option of going into government with them. We had long agonising discussions which culminated in our big Mansion House debate. This was the most open, searing and honest debate. We didn't know what our members were going to do. We were quite prepared to go in there and be told they didn't want us to go into government. But our members gave us a resounding 86 per cent mandate to go into government. So we find ourselves in this extraordinary position. People say, 'Oh, you shouldn't have gone in with Fianna

Fáil,' or, 'You will be tainted,' or, 'You should have gone into opposition,' but we are a political party and we were given a chance. I often think that if we had passed up this opportunity because we were fearful of losing our seats at Dáil or local authority level, we really shouldn't be a political party at all, we should be a campaigning protest group.

This is a unique opportunity to put into practice the policies that have been in the in-tray for twenty-six years. We are nobody's watchdog. We are going to try to 'green' the government and the country as much as we can, given the ratio of our six TDs to Fianna Fáil's seventy-eight. But we got a very good deal for government and I don't accept the criticism that it was a bit of a wimpish deal. I think as we move forward you can see what the Green ministers have done. I am very confident that we will roll out more policies so that people will say at the end of the period, 'My goodness the Greens were good in government,' not, 'My goodness, the Greens shouldn't have gone into government.' That is my hope and aspiration.

I am not afraid of the future. I would hate to come to the end of a term of government and say, 'I should have been bolder, I should have done x, y and z, I really should have enjoyed this term more.' So every day that passes here in Dáil Éireann is a fantastic opportunity, particularly for me, a rural TD in a very small party, who spent ten years trying to get in. It was extraordinary really that a Green Party member was elected in such a conservative constituency. So my focus is to keep healthy and well and deliver the goods locally. I have a reputation for working extremely hard. People kept saying to me on the doorstep, 'We know you'll work.' I think I owe my work ethic to my family background.

I served in the European Parliament and in all political Parties there is savage infighting. I saw it right across the board and right across countries and the Greens had very savage internal rows. Would that characterise your experience of political life in this country?
No. Absolutely not.

But you would be aware of it in other countries?
Oh yes. That is not to say that we don't have hugely argumentative discussions and polarised views. There are people in our Party who didn't want us to go into government, some of them high-profile people. Our mandate is to bring those people on board to see that it is a good thing to be in government, delivering on policy. I think a lot of the people who were upset or stridently opposed to the Party going in are now seeing what has been delivered over the short time that we have been in government. It would be my job, particularly as Deputy Leader, to go around the constituencies talking to people who might have doubts about the Greens in government and bringing them on board rather than saying, 'Gosh those troublesome little Greens over there causing us grief.'

I would be a very open conciliatory sort of person and I think because of the way we do our business in the Green Party, we have to reach consensus. At times, to the outsider, this might seem a long tortuous process, but in the end we normally get consensus. It is very empowering when you put a motion to the floor and you have for and against and everyone there, with no whips on them, pouring out of their heart their feelings about why we should or shouldn't go into government, or about policy issues. Our conventions are really lively affairs, not just dull droning on. I think it would be naïve to think that we are all singing from the same hymn sheet. We are not, but neither are we wearing armour-plated suits.

How do you feel about family privacy and about having your life exposed in public?

I remember when the first poster went up at our gate in 1997, I was absolutely horrified. My husband had put it up when I was out shopping. I couldn't believe that I was there at the gate and he said, 'Five hundred have gone up this morning; you'd better get used to it.' For the following election there were a thousand. So you do get used to it. Now I have, for the first time ever, a constituency office which isn't my home, in Carlow town. I think that is a great benefit for the family, because people do claim you and pop into your house. We had someone who came in on Christmas Day and had a bit of a rant. I asked him if he would like a turkey sandwich, and off he went with one.

The family does need the space even though we are a small family, and we are all very protective of one another. It is an irritant if you have no time to yourself. I am trying to deflect more of my constituents to the office but people in the immediate locality do pop in and I will always see them. At the weekend and particularly on Sunday they try not to bother you.

I have had to work at distancing myself a little because I have the habit of working too hard and you never get to the end of it. So you might as well put in the best systems, so that you can have quality delivery of service to your constituents and quality of home life as well. I find it useful to park the car around the back.

How many people have you working with you?

I have two constituency secretaries, one in Kilkenny and one in Carlow. I am dividing that post. I got as many votes in Kilkenny as Carlow. I have a very good parliamentary assistant who works in the Dáil with me. The Greens have one of the strongest constituency groups in Ireland in Carlow-Kilkenny. There are about 130 people in our local group, always ready to leaflet and fundraise and come to my aid when necessary. At a point in the campaign when the polls were ebbing and we could feel it slip away, we had enough people to knock on doors and rescue the vote.

Nuala Ahern was a close friend of mine in the European Parliament. Have you many close friends in politics?

Nuala is a very good friend of mine as well, and has been more than supportive to me over the years and very good with her cool level-headed advice. I think you need just a few close friends.

Do you have friends outside politics?

I do, but I don't see them very often. They keep me in check with emails. I have school friends with whom I still keep in touch although they are all living abroad. In fact I had an email the other day from someone I haven't seen since I left school. She said, 'I can't believe you have been elected. You were so this, that and the other at school and now there you are.' So we are going to meet up again.

What did she mean by 'this, that and the other'?

Well I was very athletic at school and she wouldn't have been. I think if you are good at sport at boarding school it is a great outlet because you go all over the place. I was pretty good at hockey and got on a lot of inter-provincial teams. One of the first cards I got when I was elected was from some of the nuns in the Ursuline Convent in Waterford, who were delighted that I got in. I really do owe them an enormous debt because they were so far-thinking in those days when I was at school in the late 1960s. They were brilliant: there was music in Waterford; there was bridge; there were golf lessons. It's amazing how advanced they were.

Was there public speaking?

Yes, but I didn't go in for that at school. I found that voice in Trinity when I was campaigning on various issues. I was one of the founders of the English Society. We did a lot of debating on texts and novels and things like that. I loved that and eventually went into publishing. I then went to work for the Spanish Cultural Institute and that involved a lot of Spanish.

When you say you went into publishing, what sort of publishing?

I worked for a firm who brought out lots of magazines, *Ireland of the Welcomes* and various other magazines. I was doing editing and writing, which I really loved, and it was great training for being in politics because I can write a speech quite quickly. I can scan a document very quickly and pick up salient points and that is from proofreading and learning how to put my thoughts together very quickly. If you are told by your boss that he wants a article by 4.30, and it is now 4.10, it's good training.

Was your husband working in this business?

No, he wasn't. He is a mathematician and we met at Trinity. But to go back to the publishing, I once edited the *Shell Guide to Ireland*, the A–J section, so I know about everything in Ireland from A–J and nothing from K–Z. The highest buildings, the biggest lakes, the smallest town – everything A to J. I had to write those little definitions and it was maddening but it was hilarious. It gave me a flair for writing. One of the people I worked for told me that I should write as I speak. Many people who are writing speeches just write them and they are not writing them as they are speaking. The art is to write as you speak. If you can get that I think you can be quite persuasive when speaking and it was a good thing to know that I could do that. Needless to say I was not thinking politics in those days.

My husband and I set up a book business called Books Unlimited. We did very simple research: we put a red dot in Dublin where all the bookshops were and there was nothing north of the Liffey. We now have five bookshops north of the Liffey. We have a big online bookstore, booksunlimited.ie. The online business is really taking off so we may downsize some of our retail shops. Some of them are in big shopping centres and rents are enormous so we are building up the online store. My husband still works in that but I haven't been in the book business for seven or eight years now.

What does your daughter do?

She is planner. She did geography and philosophy in Trinity and has just finished a Masters in planning and urban renewal, in Scotland. She's working for Edinburgh City Council.

Do you think she will come back and go into politics?

She will definitely come back. On the night of the election count she and I were sitting in the car playing our CD of Johnny Cash and we had just had a very nice Italian meal and it looked like I wasn't going to get in. My husband was inside doing the tally and she said, 'I am never going into politics, I cannot stand it,' and I said, 'Yes, you are probably right.' Then the news came through that I was going to get in and she said, 'Oh well, some day I might.' At the moment it is planning. She is only newly qualified.

What do you hope to be remembered for?

I would like to be remembered for being able to put my thoughts across in a very natural way. For speaking from the gut. For being passionate about Green Party politics. I have a very strong work ethic coupled with a keen sense of the ridiculous, a sense of humour that gets me into trouble at times. Ultimately I would like to be remembered for having broken the mould for the Party by getting elected in a rural constituency and for making a difference in Carlow-Kilkenny. I was the first woman ever elected in the constituency. Pride is one of the seven deadly sins, but I am proud of that!

Do you think that because the Greens have a strong ideological base they can be more persuasive about ideas than Fianna Fáil, Fine Gael or Labour.

We are an unusual party because of where we come from. We are very passionate about what we believe in and that has to remain true with us right through this period of government. We are policy-driven, there is no question about it, and the policies are based on the urgent need to decarbonise this country and set Ireland on a new course. Really – it is a trite expression and everyone has latched on to it – it is all about a better quality of life. If you have good food, clean water, warm safe housing, good schools and good public transport and you cherish the air we breathe and the natural environment, it is a good old recipe. So you can put that together in a cogent number of policies and sell it to the electorate in a non-preachy way.

Sometimes Greens have been very – not preachy – but very high-minded. Not that we are in any way less high-minded now, but we have to be able to turn what we have believed in for the past twenty-six years into practical political policies. I think we are much more clued into that than political dynasties are. We were the Ecology Party originally and then we became the Green Party. The Greens are allied, as you know, to Green Parties all over the world and I don't know how many of us are now in government.

This simple movement has a simple charismatic message and it mustn't be diluted but it must be wrapped up a bit. People now are clued into global warming, safe food, GM-free food, the slow food movement, energy-efficient housing and public transport. So we have to make sure that we can deliver the programme for government on those key policies. It is not just an environmental movement; we are a keen political Party. We want to drive home the things that are best for our country: that is what motivates us. We really are a motivated group of people.

How do you think you compare with the other political parties?

Well, I respect all of them. They all have their own ideology and their own founding fathers. We are not saying we are better than any of them but we have kept the passion. I think if you don't have the passion you become very bland. You become so super-smooth, with all your gurus around you and your spin doctors, that you lose the edge and the bite. I am always telling my Green colleagues that we have to continue to be passionate about what we do. We must not get complacent: we have to drive it on and keep driving it on. If we don't, we'll get stale and tired. I think this has affected some Parties, which I am not going to name. Certainly some Parties are jaded and not getting the new recruits and the vibrant young body of membership. That is the telltale thing for us. Since 14 June 2007, we have attracted more than 500 new members, which is massive.

Mary Banotti (Interviewed by John Fanagan)

Where did your name, Mary, come from?

I was the eldest of six and it was fairly predictable and usual at the time that the eldest in the family would be called Mary.

Your family has close connections with Michael Collins. How important was that when you were growing up?

When I was in my teens, I realised the significance of some of the things I had experienced as a child. For example, I would stay with my grandparents as a treat, as the eldest in the family, and I was conscious of shadows and of sadness about something, but I wasn't too clear about what it was. It wasn't until many years later that I realised that this was only a couple of years after de Valera had refused to allow anyone to attend with my grandfather at the placing of the Celtic Cross on Michael Collins's grave in Glasnevin.

It must be a great satisfaction to you, as it is to many people, that Michael Collins's grave is always covered in flowers.

Of course, yes. That is because Michael Collins had two great admirers from America who left money in a local flower shop, along with instructions that there would always be flowers on his grave.

When did the idea of a political career occur to you?

It never occurred to me, because there were no women in Irish politics, apart from the historical heroines like Maud Gonne and Countess Markievicz. I think I really became political in the broadest sense when I was in America in the 1960s. I had been there only a couple of months when Kennedy was assassinated and then there was the Civil Rights Movement. From America I went to Africa and again there was a huge amount of what was then known as 'consciousness-raising' about race and colour, and I suppose I saw how interesting it was to be involved in an issue, a wider issue. And there were also the worldwide divisions caused by the Vietnam war.

You returned to Ireland in traumatic personal circumstances. I wonder did that have anything to do with your later entry into politics?

Soon after my daughter was born in Rome, my marriage ended and Tania was abducted. When she was returned to me after two weeks I had to come home to Ireland. I had been away from Ireland for nearly fifteen years, so I knew very little about what was happening in the country. When I came back I got a job and I had a baby to rear. About a year and a half later I was so outraged about something that was happening politically that I went down and joined the Clontarf branch of Fine Gael where I found a group of elderly attendees; I was their 'youth wing' by about twenty years! I had an amazing bit of good luck because an election was called within ten days. Branch meetings of a political party tend to be dreary affairs: they are mostly about fundraising. But if one is thrown into an election it is great fun and absolutely fascinating. I was hooked from then on.

The Sunday before you were elected to the European Parliament you said to me, 'I can't stand up there again and be a gallant loser.' What would you have done if you hadn't been elected?

Well, I had been labelled 'gallant loser of the year' by the *Irish Independent* before I ran for the European elections in June 1984. I knew that I wouldn't have another chance. I had to make the choice, like many aspiring politicians, between my day job and my political ambitions. Luckily I was elected in 1984 but the day I was defeated in the 1983 by-election was certainly difficult. I did learn one very important lesson on that occasion: don't show your disappointment in public. You are gracious, you don't burst into tears, you don't say anything negative about your opponents and you go home and shed your tears in private. I was lucky: I had good friends who helped and supported me. But I was so worn out I had to spend two weeks in hospital after it. That has been a characteristic of all the interviews I have done for this book: the immediate bond I formed with the other women in politics is that we all know how truly appalling elections can be and what they take out of you.

Why would they be worse for women than for men?

I don't know that they necessarily are but I think women tend to take personally what they perceive as the slights, the deviousness and the other negative aspects.

What memories do you have, good and bad, of when you got elected after that first European campaign?

I remember waking up and it was a lovely sunny day down here in Ringsend and, lying in bed, saying, 'Holy God, I am a member of the European Parliament. What do I do now.' But I also thought that I was on my way and it was a lovely feeling. Various friends called. Then about five days later someone sent me a telegram saying, 'Come to Brussels.' I was so relieved because I thought nothing was ever going to happen.

You mentioned the bond you felt with the women you interviewed. Which of the Marys did you particularly like.

Well I know this sounds like I am kicking for touch but I really liked all of them. There were no Fine Gael women apart from myself. The majority were Fianna Fáil, plus one each Labour, Green and Sinn Féin and I expected that I might come up against a certain degree of reluctance on their part to speak to me but I assured them all that I was not there to do a hatchet job. I wanted to find out how they got from there to here and about their backgrounds. And without exception I think they are courageous. Some had easier times than others. Some had come out of tragedy. The impressive Mary Coughlan was just finishing college when she succeeded her father, who had died unexpectedly. There she was at twenty-one, a young girl in the Dáil surrounded by a lot of men who were much older. As she says herself, she was younger than some of their daughters and there she was, a TD.

As I say, I liked them all. I wouldn't really single out anyone. But I think of how consistently brave and tough someone like Mary Harney is, under constant scrutiny. She is probably under more pressure than anyone else in the current government or indeed in the previous government but she can still deliver her message with a touch of humour and irony.

Who in your time in Fine Gael politics have you particularly admired and liked?

I suppose, like all the women in Fine Gael, I admired Garret

FitzGerald because Garret, quite genuinely, hasn't a single sexist bone in his body and, without making any big deal out of it, he was determined that women were going to be part of whatever was going on in the Party. He supported you in a nice grandfatherly way. You had a feeling that Garret – and I don't mean this in a pejorative way – didn't see any difference between men and women. But he noticed that there were fewer women in politics than there were men and he was, in every sense of the word, an inspiring leader.

I didn't know John Bruton very well when he was Taoiseach but I have got to know him better since. He is very bright and funny and passionate about politics. I have met him several times in Washington and he is clearly doing a thorough job there for the EU. They would be two former leaders that I like. I am also fond of Enda Kenny and I think he has achieved a great deal in bringing the party back from the 2002 election disaster. And of course I admire my sister Nora and I know exactly what she has gone through in her political life. That's one of the great supports I have had – a sister who can share what you're going through. And she says the same.

You talked about the profile of the Dáil for someone like Mary Coughlan or Nora, going into it with so many middle-aged males. Was it the same when you joined your colleagues in the European Parliament in 1984 or was it more female, more youthful?

Oh, they were all men, I was the only Fine Gael woman and Eileen Lemass was from Fianna Fáil. There were six of us elected for Fine Gael and we had a very successful election. The older men were real gents, like Tom O'Donnell and the wonderful Mark Clinton. Mark was quite bemused by me but to his amazement we became really good friends. He was quite conservative – he would have been very much old-school – but there was something fine and noble about Mark. Tom O'Donnell is another conservative male but full of charm. I liked both of them a lot.

When I went to Brussels my political group, the EPP [European People's Party], was one of the biggest and it was predominantly male. The women in it were elected from the list systems in the countries they came from. They would not have had anything like the same electoral campaigns we had, and there wasn't a single woman in the Parliament under the age of forty-five. There were many well-known older women who had fought the good fight during the Second World War. That was a characteristic of the first session, 1984-89. I found that interesting because their memories went back to before the time I was born and most emphatically they had memories of the Second World War. These were raw and painful memories, very real in their lives. That gave them a massive commitment to making the Parliament work, because they never wanted to see people suffering so much again.

The first summer I was in the Parliament I drove my own car down to the south of France and we went through little French villages, all with war memorials. I thought of them when there were debates here about neutrality. For some reason, when I saw how many people from every French hamlet had died in wars, it gave me the kind of determination and commitment to Europe that I have to this day.

What about your first speech in Irish and your clash with Lady Ellis? I recall that Ian Paisley gave you some advice early on in your career as an MEP.

Well, the first week we were in Strasbourg, Ireland had the Presidency so someone in the Fine Gael group was going to get speaking time. Everyone wanted it so our names were put in a wine glass and mine was pulled out. I was thrilled. Altiero Spinelli, aged seventy-nine, an Italian MEP, had said to the late journalist, John Healy, 'We had great hopes for the Irish but they sent us little grey men who spoke English badly,' which was not a very nice thing to say about us! So I thought, well, I'll show him that I am not a little greybeard and I can speak Italian. So I decided then that I should also speak a little Irish. Now I knew nothing then about the procedures of the Parliament, let alone the official language policy. I stood up and in the Chair was Lady Ellis, a British member, very tough in that role. She heard this new member, a woman with an Italian name, speaking a language she had never heard and she went berserk and started banging her gavel and telling me to stop.

It is not often that you have exciting occasions in the chamber of the European Parliament. John Hume jumped up to defend me, as did the Duke of Waterloo and finally Winnie Ewing from the Scottish Isles. So we had a lovely row going and by the time I came out of the chamber I was a kind of heroine.

Shortly afterwards, I met Ian Paisley for the first time on a flight out to Strasbourg. He liked to sit in the front seat of the plane and so do I. Initially I was a bit wobbly at the knees to find myself sitting beside him. We got chatting and he was very nice to me always. It was he who told me about the official language policy. He also seemed to know exactly what vote I had got in the election and said, 'I'm glad I am not running against you,' which was enormously flattering and I was pleased as one is at the beginning when people say encouraging things to you.

I soon became aware that all the Members had heard about my maiden speech because, I think, they liked the idea that someone had taken on Lady Ellis in the Chair. In fact, as it happened, Lady Ellis later became a friend and, to this day, she always sends me a Christmas card. She had a sense of humour although not while in the Chair. Our first encounter thus brought me a certain amount of – shall we say – notoriety, which got me started, and that was very welcome.

You spent twenty years in the European Parliament and in your last election you topped the poll in Dublin. How do you think the profile of the Parliament and Europe has changed since you were first elected in 1984?

I suspect there will always be a knowledge gap between the European Parliament and the people back home, although perhaps not so much in France because the Parliament sits there (Strasbourg) as well as in Belgium (Brussels). In Ireland, you are constantly trying to bridge that gap. There are lots of bright young people who *are* interested in the mechanics of the Parliament but regrettably most people are not. So what makes the Parliament live for them, in this country anyway, is how their MEPs communicate information to them. For example, I did a lot of quite technical work in committee on the pharmaceutical industry, on the environment and on culture policy. Well, people's eyes just glaze over when you speak to them in technical terms, so you have to communicate in more human terms.

When I was elected we had the lowest level of environmental awareness in the whole of Europe. So, I set out to try to bring the environment to people's attention, with, for example, issues like air pollution and – the big thing in 1984 – acid rain, which was annihilating the forests in Germany and throughout Central Europe. Nobody had ever heard of acid rain here and they couldn't have cared less because it wasn't affecting us.

But by 1989 some of the big issues, for example water pollution, vividly manifested by dead fish in rivers here, suddenly began to impact. People generally began to wake up to the fact that, even though we weren't inheriting the same kind of environmental problems as experienced, say, by the Danube countries, we had our own problems and we needed to start doing something about them. I am really pleased, after two decades, that there is now a much higher level of environmental awareness in Ireland.

Therefore, I think it is some measure of success, for a working politician, if you have become identified with even a couple of issues that people can understand and sympathise with and in this way convey what the European Parliament was all about. I would like to think that I have been able to communicate reasonably coherently on environmental protection and child abduction issues at least.

How do you see the referendum on the Lisbon Treaty which will be held in 2008? We are the only country that will definitely be having a referendum. Are you concerned and will you be campaigning?

Yes, I will be campaigning and yes, I *am* concerned. Since I was first elected as an MEP our country has improved radically, principally as a result of our EU membership. During that period the EU has enlarged considerably and therefore become more complex. My concern is that there is a band of negative campaigners who will surface *en masse* as soon as the date of the referendum is fixed. They will campaign on issues at times far removed from the issues that the Lisbon Treaty is actually seeking to change. My other concern is that the 'No' side will align themselves with MEPs from other countries belonging to the far Right as well as to the far Left. They are likely to appear in this country and seek to confuse us enough to make us vote against or at least to abstain from voting 'Yes', which it is overwhelmingly in our national interest to do.

Do you miss being an MEP?

I think that twenty years of active service is enough for anyone in politics if you want to be an energetic, communicating, enthusiastic Member. I would like to feel that if anyone assessed my life in the European Parliament this is what they would say about me.

What was your experience of running for the Irish Presidency in 1997, when about ten days beforehand it looked as if you just might win?

Well, it was very exciting. I wouldn't have run against Mary Robinson, but when I realised that she wasn't going to run I phoned John Bruton and said, 'If you are thinking of running a candidate, I'm just telling you that I would be interested in being considered.' So he said, 'OK.' That took about thirty seconds and he hung up and I hung up and that was maybe February or March 1997 and nothing happened for several months. Then he rang me again one day and said, 'Well, are you still interested?' and I said I was. One of the things Mary Robinson had done, which was an important part of her success, was that she had managed to get around the country before the election campaign started. That was something I would have liked to do but the time for that was gone. The campaign didn't really get started until September, by which time we had what one journalist referred to as the Spice Girls show. There were four women and Derek [Nally], the so-called 'decency' candidate.

It was a hugely interesting and, at the same time, traumatic campaign. I loved campaigning in the country; that was a different experience for me. The trouble with high-profile campaigns is that you never know when something is going to crawl out from somewhere. Several times during the campaign, including the second-last day, there were unexpected hitches. There was a time when I thought I might possibly win, a thought perhaps overly influenced by how I felt Dublin was going for me. In the end I was consoled by the fact that I did at least attract the majority of votes in the greater Dublin area and I had a reasonable showing throughout the rest of the country. After it was all over I did have an interesting and fulfilling role to go back to in the European Parliament. All in all, I wouldn't have missed it for the world. In the immediate aftermath I wished President-elect Mary McAleese every success and I still do. I think she has filled the office with honour and dignity and is continuing to do so.

How would you have done it differently?

Do you know, I honestly don't know, because in a campaign you become a bit like a leaf in a storm. There are people making logistical decisions that you never hear about. You just go where you are told a lot of the time. I was aware of the huge support for Fianna Fáil, of course, but I also believed that a lot of Fianna Fáil people voted for me while I was an MEP, which might explain my high vote in Dublin.

And now?

Life goes on, still interesting, still exciting and sometimes still traumatic.